AF516401

- Establishing [illegible] rural education [illegible] and [illegible] facilities to [illegible] individual and the community leading to improvement in enrolment in schools [illegible] percentages.
- Physical Games and Active Play: [illegible] development [illegible] play and [illegible] technology [illegible]
- Health and Sanitation: [illegible]
- [illegible] youth to [illegible] ownership and be flag-bearers for [illegible] communities.
- Livelihood Diversification: [illegible] life skills [illegible] Enhancing the capability of individuals through vocational training programmes so that they can be employable and become a contributing member to the family as well as to the society at large.
- Housing: A place to live, a roof to live under is a basic need of families and communities. Enhancement of other social infrastructure to villages.
- Assistance to the ultra-poor: In all [illegible] programmes [illegible] housing, school enrolment, or [illegible] livelihood promotion, SRMM makes it a point to ensure that the poorest of the poor/the marginalized [illegible] attention.

Approaches and Strategies

- Build social infrastructure—both physical infrastructure as well as soft-infrastructure (education/orientation/training) that will enable the community to sustain benefits and assume self-responsibility. Adopt an entire village and develop it to become a model village.

Integral Rural Development

About the Authors

Prof. G. Palanithurai, Former Professor, Rajiv Gandhi Chair for Panchayati Raj studies, Department of Political Science and Development Administration, Gandhigram Rural Institute – Deemed University, Gandhigram is an academic activist. All his academic, research and outreach activities are being supported by an array of funding agencies, namely the world Bank, UNDP, UNICEF, Hunger Project, SDC, DANIDA, Action Aid International, Ford Foundation, Population Foundation of India, Rajiv Gandhi Foundation, Toolkit Foundation Netherland, Ministry of Panchayati Raj and State Planning Commission. He was a visiting professor in Cologne University, Germany. He has to his credit seventy three books, 126 research articles, 112 popular articles in popular newspapers, 83 monographs published in a span of three decades. He was and is member of many advisory committees of the Government of India and Government of Tamil Nadu pertinent to local governance and rural development.

Dr R. Ramesh is working as Associate Professor at the National Institute of Rural Development & Panchayati Raj (NIRDPR), Hyderabad. He also works closely with the Ministry of Panchayati Raj and Ministry of Jal Sakthi in their training and capacity building efforts. He is associated with the Unnat Bharat Abhiyan (UBA) programme of the Ministry of Education. In UBA, Dr R Ramesh serves as a member of the Subject Expert Group, and also as a member of the National Coordination Committee of UBA Programme. His involvement in rural development spans over 30 years. He has published several books, papers and training manuals on rural development related themes. Before moving to work for NIRDPR Hyderabad, he worked for Sri Aurobindo Society, Puducherry for a brief period.

Integral Rural Development

A Rural Transformation Experiment
by
Sri Aurobindo Society, Pondicherry

[Revised and Enlarged Edition]

G. Palanithurai
R. Ramesh

Sri Aurobindo Society
AUROPUBLICATIONS
POWERFUL THOUGHTS, INSPIRING VISION

Concept
Since 1974

CONCEPT PUBLISHING COMPANY PVT. LTD.
NEW DELHI - 110059

Published and Printed by
Concept Publishing Company Pvt. Ltd.

Regd Office:
A/15-16, Commercial Block, Mohan Garden, New Delhi-110059 (INDIA)
T: +91-11-41101460,
E: publishing@conceptpub.com, *W*: www.conceptpub.com

First Published 2015
Revised Edition 2024

ISBN: 978-93-5594-736-9

Research and Presented by

Sri Aurobindo Society
SARVAM
SRI AUROBINDO RURAL AND VILLAGE ACTION AND MOVEMENT

Published in arrangement with:
AuroPublications, Sri Aurobindo Society, Puducherry - 605 001.
Website: www.auropublications.org | www.aurosociety.org
Email: info@auropublications.org

Copyright©2024 AuroPublications

All rights reserved under international copyright conventions. No part of this book may be reproduced or transmitted in any form or by any means, electronic or mechanical, including photocopy, recording or by any other information storage and retrieval system, without prior permission in writing from the publisher.

Cataloging in Publication--Courtesy: D.K. Agencies (P) Ltd. <docinfo@dkagencies.com>

Palanithurai, G., author.
Integral rural development : a rural transformation experiment by Sri Aurobindo Society, Pondicherry / G. Palanithurai, R. Ramesh ; researched and presented by Sri Aurobindo Society, SARVAM (Sri Aurobindo Rural and Village Action and Movement). -- Revised and enlarged edition.
pages cm
Study conducted in two villages, Poothurai and Perambai in Vanur block of Villupuram District in Tamil Nadu, India.
Includes index.
ISBN 9789355947369

1. Rural development--Government policy--India--Poothurai. 2. Rural development--Government policy--India--Perambai. 3. Sri Aurobindo Society. Sri Aurobindo Rural and Village Action and Management. I. Ramesh, R., 1968- author. II. Sri Aurobindo Society. Sri Aurobindo Rural and Village Action and Management, issuing body. III. Title.

LCC HN690.Z9C6 2024 | DDC 307.1412095482 23

Foreword

The challenge of development, in its broadest sense, is to improve the quality of life. A better quality of life generally calls for higher income but it involves much more. It encompasses as ends in themselves, better education, higher standards of health and nutrition, less poverty, a cleaner environment, more equality of opportunity, greater individual freedom, a richer cultural engagement, and a fulfilling spiritual life. Undoubtedly, any notion of development must, at a minimum, look beyond growth in per capita incomes. Economic growth as such does not translate into social development or reduction of poverty level. Unless standard of living and quality of thinking of people improve, development will be lopsided or only an illusion.

A common growth has no meaning unless a woman or man finds an increase in her/his household income and access to common facilities and services is improved. The concept of integral development aims at raising the consciousness level of individuals and families, and in the process, the economic necessities must be attended to as well. It is more about shaping the values and principles of dignified living—practicing the principles of individual self-esteem and social harmony. Thus, the SARVAM Village Development Project aims at making the people move towards exploring their consciousness, and causing an awakening to the meaning of life, what we call social transformation through individual transformation.

If we trace the idea of development in the past seventy years or so, it has shifted quite often. Progress has not always moved along a straightline from darkness to light. Instead there has been a gradual accumulation of knowledge and insight. On some matters, a fairly clear understanding has emerged, but many questions still remain contentious and unanswered.

The SARVAM experiment—spiritual approach to rural development—is one of the vivid examples, where we are clear of the outcome. By and large, we have been able to realize our dream of translating integral rural development on the ground. Yet, we need to work deeper on some of the areas to be able to create a long-lasting impact. I am happy we could take up this innovative experiment.

I must thank the Cadbury, Mumbai for the generous financial support that made us step into our service villages to take up this experiment. Subsequently, other agencies such as TCS, L&TFS, HDFC, and US Embassy support us to sustain these endeavours. I must acknowledge the work of Mr. K. Senthilkumar, Ms. S. Chitra, and our volunteers in the villages for the excellent fieldwork that has translated our vision into a reality; and Prof. G. Palanithurai, Dr. Thirunavukkarasu and Dr. R. Ramesh for their help in documenting this experiment.

I am strongly of the opinion that a spiritual approach to rural development holds the key to a sustainable future. In that sense, the Village Development Project is a flagship project of the Sri Aurobindo Society, Puducherry. Mother tells us: One ounce of practice is worth tonnes of preaching. We are happy we could do something to bring about real change in the lives of over tens of thousands of families in SARVAM villages. I am happy that the Mother has made bringing out a revised and updated version of this book possible. If development professionals and practitioners could draw lessons from the SARVAM experiment in their own work, we shall be immensely pleased.

Vijay
Sri Aurobindo Society

Preface

At times I wonder if there is any other country on this planet that has experimented and put in place the range of rural development programmes and approaches that India has. As development professionals we are well-blessed to have been born in India. Diversity of India is spoken about, often in terms of language, culture, religion, terrain and so on. The variety and the diversity of rural development programmes and institutions we have in India in the last 100 years provide another dimension to the richness of this diversity.

India has, therefore, over a century of rural development experience. The approaches and strategies adopted by the programmes implemented by the Governments—Central and States, and a plethora of Civil Society Organizations or NGOs markedly vary. A country that was in a torphor of food insecurity and communicable diseases has today progressed to show the way to the rest of the world on 'e-governance, using satellite imageries and Artificial Intelligence and IoT technologies etc. not only in manufacturing but also in the rural development sector'. We have come a long way indeed. For sure, the results of India's rural development efforts are encouraging. I make this statement bearing in mind the enormity of the challenge in terms of the vastness of the country, its massive population and infinite culture and so on.

A country that was considered as not having enough to feed its population of 300 million at the time of Independence, today trains its rural population to get on to digital modes financial transactions. These are enormous achievements, but for the two year period of Corona-19 Pandemic that shock the entire world. The discussion at the moment is not about elimination of poverty as it used to be about two decades ago. It is about well-being; Ease of Living, and improving the quality of life. There is considerable change witnessed in rural economy, polity, social and agricultural dynamics. Despite significant progress made in many sectors of development, certain rural development challenges still persist. This is partly because of the 'output-orientation' many of the government programmes focus on, unmindful of the 'outcome expected'. Often times, the output is reported in financial terms as a proxy for real development, which is evidently deceptive.

SARVAM (Sri Aurobindo Rural & Village Action & Movement), the rural development unit of Sri Aurobindo Society in Pondicherry has put into practice an innovative concept in rural development which they call 'Integral Rural Development'. It fascinates me for two reasons. One, it provides a spiritual perspective to rural development practice. In other words, the approach aims at bringing about rural development that is human-spirit centric, rather than narrowing it down to the conventional economics of income enhancement *per se*. The second reason is SARVAM started implementing the concept of Integral Rural Development in two village panchayats in Villupuram district, Tamil Nadu to begin with. Now this approach has been operationalized in nearly sixty villages in the neighbourhood. It is not just a concept on paper or in mind. This experiment enticed me to make frequent visits to SARVAM villages and study what's going on—especially on the ground and in the mindsets of people. Dr. R. Ramesh and I have tried giving our understanding of this experiment, and how the transformation process took flow in two exclusive chapters here. Thus, the last two chapters summarize the lessons and key principles that emerge out of this experiment for nearly two decades now.

This is an account of the fieldworks carried out and the outcome as captured initially by Dr. M.A. Thirunavukkarasu—an independent scholar from Gandhigram; and subsequently taken up by Dr. R. Ramesh, Associate Professor at the National Institute of Rural Development & Panchayati Raj, Hyderabad. I must thank Sri Vijay Poddar of Sri Aurobindo Society for taking this initiative, and those who support and associate with SARVAM's rural development work, which has made presenting this work to a wider readership possible. Above all, I must acknowledge the participation of the people in SARVAM villages and the remarkable works carried out by Mr. K. Senthilkumar and Ms. S. Chitra and their team who are actually demonstrating the concept of Integral Rural Development into actual practice.

Prof. G. Palanithurai
Gandhigram Rural Institute—Deemed University

Contents

Village Education Committee

SARVAM believes in facilitating the community to take the responsibility to make decisions, and own whatever common assets are built. The decisions made must be through institutions that have local grounding. In each village where SARVAM works a Village Education Committee (VEC) has been formed. There are also [illegible] Teacher Association (PTA). The presence of [illegible]

[illegible] with government funds. SARVAM [illegible] the cooperation of the PTA in organizing an annual educational [illegible] children. [illegible] PTA [illegible] local [illegible] of SARVAM [illegible]

[illegible] and teachers [illegible] to play their [illegible] and create an awakening in their consciousness that before pointing the finger at others one needs to look inward into oneself. SARVAM was [illegible] to bring into play such consciousness awakening for the benefit of the children.

RE[illegible]

100[illegible] children, [illegible] students at primary and secondary level and [illegible] at high school level, 400 students from higher [illegible]

[illegible] students have learnt to use computers, and 2000 [illegible] children's corner for innovative learning.

List of Abbreviations & Acronyms

ABC	:	Activity Based Curriculum
ABC	:	Attitude and Behaviour Change
AAG	:	Auroville Action Group—A local NGO
BDO	:	Block Development Officer
CSR	:	Corporate Social Responsibility
CSRT	:	Centre for Sustainable Rural Transformation
DRDA	:	District Rural Development Agency
GoI	:	Government of India
GoTN	:	Government of Tamil Nadu
GRI	:	Gandhigram Rural Institute
IAY	:	Indira Awas Yojana
JIPMER	:	Jawaharlal Institute of PG Medical Education & Research
NIRDPR	:	National Institute of Rural Development & Panchayati Raj
NABARD	:	National Bank for Agriculture and Rural Development
NGO	:	Non-Governmental Organization
NREGS	:	National Rural Employment Guarantee Scheme
NYK	:	Nehru Yuva Kendra
PMAY-G	:	Prime Minister Awas Yojana—Gramin
PMJDY	:	Prime Minister Jan Dhan Yojana
PTA	:	Parent Teachers Association
SBM-G	:	Swachh Bharat Mission—Gramin
SHG	:	Self-help Groups
SARVAM	:	Sri Aurobindo Rural & Village Action & Movement
SSA	:	Sarva Shiksha Abhiyan
VEC	:	Village Education Committee
VP	:	Village Panchayat
SAS	:	Sri Aurobindo Society

Chapter 1

How Does Development Take Place ?

Introduction

How does development take place in a community? Researchers, academics, and social activists have been searching for answers to this question almost from the days of Adam Smith (1723-1790) and Robert Owen (1771-1858). A tag that pops up almost simultaneously is: what do we call 'development' in the first place? Some might say that it is a long term process of structural, societal transformation; others might say that it is a short-to-medium term outcome of desirable targets; and a third school might brush aside all these and say it is a dominant discourse of Western modernity or of western making.

Explanations abound depending on the worldview or standpoint of the researchers or reflective practitioners. Mahatma Gandhi had his own prescient theories for rural development. J.C. Kumarappa had his perception of, and prescriptions for rural development. Sri Aurobindo had his own view which he called 'integral development'. He says: ***The village is the cell of the national body and the cell-life must be healthy and developed for the national body to be healthy and developed ... we must begin at the bottom and work up to the apex...*** the message is to make a genuine difference not only to their way of living, but also to their way of thinking and being.

This book is the result of a dialogue between practice and reflection—reflective practice. The context is SARVAM's rural development experiments in South Indian villages. Nearly two decades ago (in 2005), this experiment set out searching for answers to an important question. That was: *How does development take place*? The question itself was as intriguing as the answer was to be. The nature and depth of this question is such that it can be compared to asking a meditative question such as: *What is the meaning of life*?

When the development approach adopted by SARVAM was explained it was fascinating to many. The reason: the method followed had a set of strategies and approaches devised deliberately away from the mainstream methods and approaches to rural development. It was called: 'Integral rural development', which aimed at transformation of physical and mental—in other words, material progress and spiritual awareness. Material progress means progressive reduction of deprivations and penury. Spiritual awareness means enhancement in the level of consciousness of oneself and their socio-physical surroundings. The simple logic is that you cannot teach upanishads to a hungry man. Sri Aurobindo believed this to be true. There must be comfortability in one's socio-physical environment, including the resources to remain hunger-free, so as to focus on development of the mind or the consciousness.

It is with this vision in mind that the Sri Aurobindo Rural & Village Action & Movement (SARVAM), a unit of Sri Aurobindo Society in India, is developing a progressive village community model that is sustainable. Now after two decades of practice SARVAM has demonstrated that it is replicable, and scalable. It works with the ideals of Sri Aurobindo—a philosopher and visionary who lived in India at the beginning of the 20th Century.

To begin with SARVAM worked in two villages, Poothurai and Perambai, in Vanur block of Villupuram district in Tamil Nadu. In the last five years or so it has extended to over sixty villages. SARVAM was established as a rural development unit of Sri Aurobindo Society in the year 2002-03. It started working in these two villages from the year 2005. All that SARVAM had while commencing work in these villages were clarity of their vision and mission and commitment to work with the community to help them realize their potentials. There was no donor supported funding or time bound project to carry out. It was started with complete faith in Sri Aurobindo's precept that ***'All the world's possibilities in man are waiting as the tree waits in its seeds'***. The vision was clear. But all that we had in hand was the seed of hope. SARVAM took off and it has been on the go for nearly twenty years now (2023). The message of Sri Aurobindo is the mission: Making a genuine difference not only to their [people's] way of living, but also to their way of thinking and being.

> Sri Aurobindo Society is an international, non-profit NGO, with its headquarters at Puducherry, working for individual perfection, social transformation and human unity. The Society has been recognized by the Government of India as a charitable organization, a research institution and an institute of national importance. The main areas of the Society's work are Integral Education, Integral Health, Integral Rural Development, Sustainable Development and Science & Technology, Integral Management, Indian Culture, Youth and Women, Media, Arts & Communication, Business & Economic Development.

This is a self-appraisal or self-anchoring exercise that we have taken up to see the transformation process at work in the past two decades that SARVAM has put into operation the idea of integral rural development. The work of SARVAM has brought about admirable changes in the community. We are delighted to notice a lot of socio-economic changes taking place in these villages, which draws visitors from various parts of the country, and beyond. We strongly feel SARVAM villages have lots to offer for rural development professionals across India and else. ***Impressed by the development milestones SARVAM had facilitated these villagers cross, a World Bank team that visited these two villages asked us what policy prescriptions we are giving the Government of Tamil Nadu for adopting SARVAM's way of working on a larger scale.*** This exercise, perhaps, must have several insights to offer that may help to find the answer to our fundamental question: **How does development take place? What approaches and strategies work? And what have we to offer to development practitioners and the larger development community as lessons learnt or best practices from this experiment?** Although the answer we get could be context-specific, it should throw light on certain thumb-rules for scaling up.

The first point is about our approach to understanding and explaining development. Development is progressive, and it must be measured in terms of improvement in the quality of life of rural people. It must be viewed in terms of enabling ease of living, and enhancing the capability of people for self-propulsion. The process adopted should facilitate raising the level of consciousness among the community we work with. Therefore, development should take place like a steady flow of mild rain seeping into the ground, augmenting groundwater.

It cannot be like a wild rain washing down the streets into drainage ultimately to join the gutter. Simply, rural development entangled with politics is disempowering. For a policy prescription to be viewed as workable, the criteria are: administrative feasibility; political desirability and fund availability. Fund is not a constraint for a willing government. The real constraint very likely to be is the idea of disentangling rural development from politics. Administrative machinery can be set right through social audit and other processes.

India—given the diversity—cannot have a single approach to rural development. Nor can we make a statement that an approach that does not contribute to policy is not worth pursuing. Some experiments may be able to contribute to policy; others may contribute to literature; yet others may contribute to improvised development practice and so on. Our purpose here is to present another approach to rural development, which is rarely experimented and documented—i.e. spiritual approach. We call it Integral Approach to Rural Development.

Humans as biological (physical) being have evolved. They have a plethora of physical needs, which are basically for the survival process. There are many government programmes that cater to such survival needs. Human nature is such that needs grow into wants—wants grow into greed. There is always a search—an endless search. Be it a family or nation there is a constant comparison with our neighbours taking note of relative deprivation. Most of these are physical or survival needs. They also have an emotional element to it.

For humans to evolve as super humans as envisioned by Sri Aurobindo we need to move towards finding that element of fulfilment or self-awareness. This is discovering another great dimension to human life. This is moving towards an evolved self, and being able to come to terms with harmony with oneself, and his surroundings.

In other words, it is our transactions with the social world of nearby communities and the larger society; and the natural world of soil, plants, animals and other species. This is about responsible well-being with the society and the nature. Such an evolved human is called a transformed individual—thus, the expression 'transformed community, transformed society' etc. We shall elaborate more about this approach as we go into explaining the works of SARVAM. Thus, development is not merely about physical or a survival process. It is also about mental and finding that element which enables fulfilment. It is about having an evolved mindset to live in harmony and peace with the society and nature.

Writing this book is an exercise in reminiscence—a reminiscent journey of SARVAM's work down the line. A projection of knowledge about the present into the past, at least tells us how the past was and what changes have been brought about through our development interventions. We can describe the essential characteristics of the dynamics of households in a host of SARVAM villages.

Purpose of this Book

- To have a written record of activities, events and processes that have taken place in about sixty villages where this experiment was carried out in Tamil Nadu and Puducherry.
- To stand witness to the transformation that has taken place in SARVAM villages and the contribution of various institutions and strategies that made it possible.
- To obtain certain basic principles (or broad lessons) that may help stretching out to more villages, the best practices and lessons learnt from this experiment.
- To draw ideas that may contribute to the literature on spiritual approach to rural development that might be of interest to development professionals, NGOs, researchers and others.

Rural Transformation—What Difference does it Make?

What SARVAM attempted was not to bring about 'rural development' in the conventional sense of the term. It aims at 'rural transformation'. We must understand it like this: Development can be sector-specific and compartmentalized but 'transformation' transcends sectors, and cuts across sectors. In other words, development generally aims at fulfilling the material needs of rural persons or households so that they are facilitated to get out of a poverty threshold usually fixed from outside.

Transformation aims at transcending the material needs of persons, and makes efforts to bring about changes in the way a person thinks and acts so that she/he takes charge of what kind of material

and spiritual changes shell he personally aspires to achieve or values the most and not by yardsticks determined from outside the community. Development could be sector specific or integrated. Transformation that is integral transcends and touches upon one's thinking, doing and being. Therefore, although the prime purpose is documenting SARVAM's experiment in the field and weighing the merits of the model for scaling up, it has a lot of conceptual/theoretical interests as well.

A Brief Note on the Two Villages

Study of a community should start from a careful analysis of vital social and economic data concerning the individuals and families making up the community being studied. Besides this, there are other factors coming into play such as village governance, institutions at work and so on. There are also less measurable data on attitudes, cultural traits, faiths, behaviour patterns in which societal stratification is expressed. This is more so in Tamil Nadu villages where multi-caste communities including the Scheduled Caste people co-reside. Let us take a look at the two villages, where SARVAM began work. This may give a perspective of state of life and livelihoods in these villages, and what transformational process SARVAM could set in motion.

Villupuram in Tamil Nadu State in southern India, was one of the worst affected by the Tsunami, and is in great need of developmental support and help. In Villupuram, the largest district in Tamil Nadu, lie Poothurai and Perambai. These two adjacent villages, forming one unit, are about 15 kms from Pondicherry. Major community groups belong to the Scheduled Caste (SC) or Vanniar, which is an MBC (Most Backward Caste). These villages are very typical, representing all the problems, difficulties, challenges, and also opportunities of most villages in Tamil Nadu or even in India for that matter. These two Village Panchayats have seven hamlets within them and they have a total population of 7000, making up 1300 households—good enough to take up any rural development experiment.

SARVAM is supposed to actualize the concept of integral rural development as ground reality. The bottom line is impacting on a person's way of thinking and being, rather than ending up with providing some essentials for improving living standards, although it is necessary and cannot be ignored. It should also take cognizance of remaining relevant to contemporary reality, people's mindset, external influences, and the way the larger world works. SARVAM's village development programme was initiated and is being implemented by the Sri Aurobindo Society from the year 2005.

The Framework

This is not a mere documentation or chronicle of activities carried out in SARVAM villages. It is about events and processes as well, and attempt to explain what happened, why it happened, and the way it happened.

The processes of transformation and the integral nature of development that SARVAM envisions is what singles out the SARVAM experiment from the conventional rural development practices. Therefore, the framework must consider the development ideals which SARVAM claims as unique, plus the institutions that have been roped into play, and how the transformation has been operationalised as development practice. These lessons must serve as lessons for other development practitioners. The outcome of this operational process is what we call the transformation brought about in the two villages in 2005, or twenty villages in 2023 as the case may be. This is what this researcher has as a mental-map to capture and report about. This is given at the outset in order to present the data and the relevant narrative in order.

Methodology and Fieldwork

Certain methods of development research have been used in preparation of this document. The approach to presentation is mostly narrative. Since this is an experiment intended for scaling up, Appreciative Enquiry has been extensively used. These emerge from the personal accounts of persons who have benefited from SARVAM's services in these villages, a chain of interviews and direct observations made on the spot. The researcher has no personal connections with the two villages, and so gaining entry was possible only through the field workers who have been in these villages for quite some years.

Besides doing a desk review of reports of various projects implemented and annual reports published, this researcher made several visits to these twenty villages. This helped capture various facets of village life, and to record the events and transformation processes from the perspective of each one involved. A series of plausible stories have been written down as well. These will be presented in boxes so that it serves the purpose of corroboration to what is being written up in the main text.

In essence this is learning from the field. Still this researcher would consider the answers tentative however convincing they may appear. The reason is our sample Village Panchayats are only twenty compared to the size of the state or country for that matter. We do not intent to make policy prescriptions for in the State of Tamil Nadu with over 12,620 inhabited villages. The lessons from here could be experimented on a relatively larger scale either within the state or in neighbouring states, before we go for policy prescriptions for the entire state or nation. However, as of now, our purpose is not policy prescription. But this study shall, for sure, come out with 'best practice notes' and lessons for grassroots level replication.

Data Collection Techniques

Basically there are three techniques of data collection we could use in this kind of study: (i) eliciting verbal responses through interviewing informants in an informal way, with or without the aid of an interview guide; (ii) observing the behaviour, sometimes as participant observer and at other times as a non-participant onlooker; and (iii) analysing documents available with SARVAM Project office or private individuals, for example, an official letter received by a community member etc. These are the methods used for data collection. We have gone in for less of quantification and more of events and life-history

narration—and deliberately so. ***A principle in development/sociological research is: 'Let us make the important quantitative and not the quantitative important'.***

The purpose is to capture 'results and lessons', and not the 'output' *per se*. The researchers have also used some standard tools for measuring perceived well-being of the community, and happiness of the children in the project villages. It happens often, the focus of investigation changing as the researcher interacts in the field. What is considered important is flexibility and ability to respond to the demands of the field situation, rather than sticking to a fixed questionnaire. All said and done, necessarily there should be appropriate fit between the nature of the community being investigated and the techniques of data collection.

As an outsider doing this study for SARVAM, there is a need to be sensitive not to injure the way SARVAM has been treating the community members. Therefore, ***we have treated the community members as 'co-researchers' in this process, rather than as 'subject matter' being studied. One example of this is calling the plausible stories collected from the field as 'life-histories' and NOT 'case-studies'. An old lady selling vegetables, narrating her life-history, is not a 'case with a number tag' for us to investigate.***

She is a human being with emotions, volunteering to share her personal stories with us, without ever questioning how we shall use her information. This also brings in the imperative of researcher-integrity and ethics in development research.

Analysis and Presentation

This is making an interpretation of the larger meaning of the data or obtaining a general sense of the information. Since the study was designed to be primarily qualitative, no statistical tools were employed. Therefore, the data analysis procedure followed is from among the qualitative research convention which required continual reflection about the data while the study was on-going in the field, asking analytic questions in line with the framework of evaluation set out. We needed to analyse it for issues, themes and perspectives, generating categories of information, while positioning it within the development ideals of SARVAM. It helped generation of meaning units, and the development of essence description, and subsequent explanation from the perspective of Integral Rural Development. Meaning derived from a few life-histories, retelling the participants' stories in the actual plot and setting them as 'boxes' in this report have been done to enhance readability. After the first draft of the book we had to go for validating the accuracy of the findings so as to demonstrate the reliability of procedures and discuss scalability.

This book is presented in seven chapters:

Chapter 1: Presents a framework to understand what is covered in this document, the purpose of this report, and the methodology adopted in preparing this document.

Chapter 2: This is a brief account of SARVAM, as a unit of Sri Aurobindo Society in Pondicherry, its vision, mission, and the values it upholds.

Chapter 3: This is a complete narration of the programmes SARVAM has implemented in Poothurai and Perambai at the beginning of this experiment, along with cases of families and individuals who have greatly benefited through SARVAM's intervention. In brief these are the activities of SARVAM.

Chapter 4: This chapter presents the key lessons from the SARVAM experiment—what SARVAM has to offer in terms of development practices to other development practitioners or to development literature.

Chapter 5: This chapter is about sustainability of activities, perceptions of self and the social of families involved in SARVAM's experiment presented as sustainability and replicability.

Chapter 6: The idea of responsible well-being and the joy of working with women and children are presented. This section also has a quick survey of perceived well-being of households, and of children associated with SARVAM.

Chapter 7: Prof. G. Palanithurai from Gandhigram Rural Institute—Deemed University, who has been involved in SARVAM's experiment almost from the beginning, gives his understanding and explanation of how the rural transformation has taken place.

Chapter 2

A Brief Account of SARVAM

Establishment

The SARVAM Village Programme was started by Sri Aurobindo Society in 2005 to carry out research-oriented outreach programmes on rural transformation. Sri Aurobindo Society is a not-for-profit organisation (NGO), working throughout the world for individual perfection, social transformation, and human unity in diversity. It is registered as a society at Kolkata (India), under the Societies Registration Act of 1860 (now West Bengal Act XXVI of 1961). The main administrative office of the Society is in Pondicherry. The Society works primarily in the areas of Education, Leadership & Management, Indian Culture & Rural Development and is recognized by the Government of India as:

- A Not-for-profit Organization under Section 80G of the Indian Income Tax Act;
- A Research Institute under Section 35(1)(iii); and
- An Institution of National Importance under Section 10(23C) (iv).

SARVAM started its activities after adopting two villages, Poothurai and Perambai, along with their seven constituent hamlets, in Villupuram district of Tamil Nadu. In assessing the past achievements and future potential of SARVAM, it is useful to clarify and give details of the development ideals, development institutions and development practices that SARVAM follows. 'Integral rural development' is the basic precept of SARVAM.

Development that transcends socio-economic well-being of individuals and goes further to touch upon the emotional/spiritual side of a person (and thus of a community) to enable them lead a life that she/he values the most and which gives shape to her/his inner-self, is basically called 'integral development'. In that sense, it cuts across the sector-specific boundaries of development to bring about 'rural transformation'. ***The word 'integrated' goes with the concept of development; whereas 'integral' goes with the concept of transformation.*** Thus, you will find the concept of 'transformation' frequently used in SARVAM's reporting, rather than development *per se*.

We shall see the features of integral development and how it is different from 'integrated development' in the later part of this book. In brief, SARVAM considers integrated development sector-specific and materialistic. It has very little to do with consciousness or inner-self of community members. SARVAM believes that if rural transformation has to take place, we need to go beyond the sector boundaries within which development is often discussed. When that is done you get the larger picture of the process at work. We need to be process-oriented in our approach to work rather than making a materialistic delivery of certain facilities for the desirable change to take place. For this to happen, the attitude and behaviour of the facilitators matter too.

In order to give meaning to the kind of development SARVAM aims at, it works with certain ideals, such as making efforts to bring about genuine and lasting change in not only people's way of living, but also in their thinking and being. That's at the ideal or conceptual level but for these ideals to translate into development practice there must be functioning institutions, especially local ones, in place.

These institutions act as the facilitating media for useful community action to take place. These could be Panchayats, local schools, cooperatives, youth clubs, children's clubs, self-help groups and so on. SARVAM thus plays the 'instrumental role' for rural transformation to take place. It has taken up translating the integral development on the ground in reality.

The bottom line is impacting on the person's way of thinking and being, rather than just providing some essentials for supporting the survival needs or improving the incomes or living standards. It should also take cognizance of remaining relevant to contemporary reality, people's mindset, external influences, and the way the larger system works.

SARVAM's approach lays a special emphasis on research and training, and works towards a sustainable, replicable and scalable model, for India as well as for other rural and developing communities in the rest of the world.

Vision

A strong, enlightened, prosperous and progressive India—a leader in the ways of spirituality, a friend and helper of all the people.

In this vision both rural and urban communities will be equally developed and play their true and complementary roles in building a new India, united and rich in its diversity.

Mission

- Initiate a movement for an integral village development, which aims at establishing and developing a progressive and happy village community, empowered and directed from within, and based on a new consciousness, attitudes and values.
- Integrate and try to bring harmony and perfection in every aspect of village life, based on a spiritual approach.
- Help every individual of the village, without any division of the village community based on age, gender, caste or religion, to realize her/his highest physical, emotional, mental and spiritual potential.

Principles and Values

The following are some of the basic principles and development values SARVAM believes in as the basis for change. In fact, these make SARVAM a unique experiment in development practice.

- **Change in Consciousness:** People aspiring towards better conditions of life should 'be ready to take up responsibilities' and they must understand the fundamental need for a change in their attitude and consciousness.
- **Harness the Potentials of Self-reliance:** Development can take place only through creating social and institutional connections where the community aspiring to change assumes main charge. In other words, community capacity, local resources and developmental aspirations should be harnessed for their own development.
- **Integral Development:** Facilitate development to take place in an integral fashion rather than touching upon isolated elements of development that might result in unintentional development distortions. In other words, facilitate integral development of villages with process-orientation, not losing sight of preparing the communities towards making right ethical discriminations.
- **Sustainable Solutions:** Our effort to achieving well-being should not end up giving additional pressure on the environment; rather it must follow the path of responsible use of resources and technologies.

The Basis for Change

The following are some of the basic tenets and development principles SARVAM believes in as the basis for change.

- Development is not presented on a platter by an outside agency, rather it is facilitated through collaboration and networking where the community involved assumes main charge. In other words, community capacity, local resources and developmental aspirations/spirit require harnessing for their own development.
- Exploring together (i.e. outside agency and community aspiring towards a dignified development) to unearth opportunities, expand choices and empower people to make use of such opportunities and choices. Information empowerment holds the key here.

- Development with dignity in an integral fashion rather than touching upon isolated elements of development that might result in unintentional development distortions. In other words, facilitate integral development of villages with process-orientation and without losing sight of the outcome, and the purpose of development.
- SARVAM's approach to development and its operational methods are different. Yet, it is designed in such a way that the end-result created shall contribute to human development elements, such as education, promotion of healthy families, expanded livelihood opportunities and decent income to people, which are in line with what the Government of India (GoI) aims at achieving.
- SARVAM stands out mainly because it activates the higher consciousness and developmental aspirations of communities. And it aligns governance systems to deliver according to the people's needs.
- Theorise development practices for wider dissemination and duplication.

Areas of Intervention

Rural transformation is composed of fulfilling: (i) social, (ii) economic, (iii) spiritual or emotional, and (iv) political well-being.

To do this, the model that SARVAM has initiated in the service villages should be disseminated and reproduced.

- **Social well-being:** Being well-nourished, well-clothed, having decent housing, quality health care and education, safe and adequate water and sanitation facilities, satisfying leisure hours and socio-cultural freedom. And other needs that people have reason to value. For example promotion of eco-friendly housing does not simply mean adhering to certain carbon emission standards but as part of promoting 'responsible well-being'.
- **Economic well-being:** This is ensured through employment and livelihood opportunities; opportunities to make choices and one's ability to enhance capabilities to make use of such opportunities. A person with many capabilities could be engaged in many different activities and pursue different life paths. This can serve as a means of overcoming financial poverty, which in turn can help a person lead a fulfilling life that he or she will value. This idea is translated

into reality through vocational training programmes, start-up assistance and offering the necessary hand-holding at the initial stages.

- **Spiritual and Emotional well-being:** This is about dignity and self-respect which are integral elements of freedom. This ignites transformation of self. This is essentially what real development is all about. The mindset of feeling uncomfortable to being recipients or beneficiaries of development can allow a person to assume a key player role in the transformation process. This lays emphasis squarely on self-reliance and finding ways to sustain development.
- **Political well-being:** They play the role of the human agency that makes governmental systems functional and development favourable to the poor. This gives shape to micro-policies and broad rules for a vibrant democracy at the grassroots level, develop a sense of participation in community activities, feel empowered to make decisions and take responsibility to carry out the programmes, initially with the guidance of SARVAM.

Sectors of Intervention

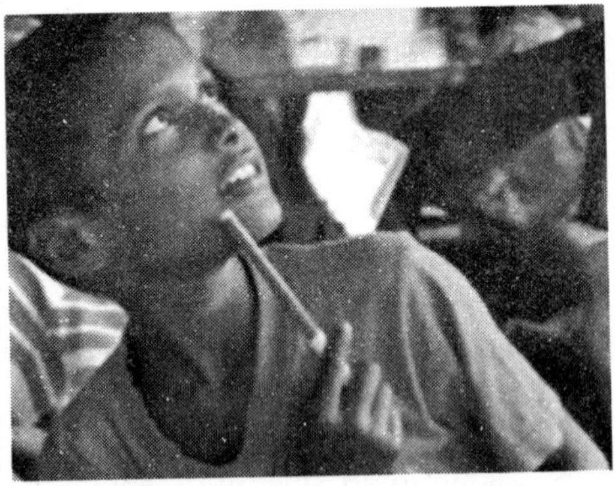

SARVAM's sectors of intervention include Education, Health, Housing, Livelihood Promotion, Media for Social change, and training and capacity building. SARVAM is a process of human and community development which unfolds from within each person, the family and community. The impact visualized encompasses material, social as well as spiritual dimensions. The programmes include the following:

- **Education and Awareness Generation:** Generating awareness of self, *vis-à-vis* the community at large, the conditions, the possibilities, the aspiration for development of the self and community, and the right ways to manifest it.

- **Establishing imperatives on formal education**, including moral and intellectual faculties in every individual of the community, leading to improvement in enrolment in schools; higher pass percentages.
- **Physical Games and Active Play:** Extension of education to develop skills in active play and sports, art, culture, media and technology resulting in overall development of children.
- **Health and Sanitation:** Communicate and generate awareness on the importance of cleanliness and hygiene for a healthy life; regular health camps for guidance, investigations and treatment; and improve sanitation facilities.
- **Women and Youth Development:** Inspiring absolute confidence in youth (men and women) to live and earn independently, and be active participants in ensuring their children's education as well as community development. In addition, inspiring and educating youth to develop skills, to take ownership and be flag-bearers for the development of their villages and communities.
- **Livelihood Diversification:** By introducing life skills and necessary training and inculcating the right attitude, mindset and respect towards work. Enhancing the capability of individuals through vocational training programmes so that they can be employable and become a contributing member to the family as well as to the society at large.
- **Housing:** A place to live; a roof to live under is a basic need of families and communities. Enhancement of other social infrastructure in villages.
- **Assistance to the ultra-poor:** In all its programmes—be it housing, school enrolment, or a revolving fund for livelihood promotion, SARVAM makes it a point to ensure that the poorest of the poor/the marginalized get priority attention.

Approaches and Strategies

- Build social infrastructure—both physical infrastructure as well as soft-infrastructure (education/orientation/training) that will enable the community to sustain benefits and assume self-responsibility. Adopt an entire village and develop it to become a model village.

- Be multifaceted, integrating all aspects of life—education, health, economic development, vocational training, organic farming, water harvesting, waste management etc. Equal and sustainable resource use.
- The project is driven internally, at every step, by the community itself, right from the planning, to the execution and the maintenance. Encourages local decision making; empowers the village community to take charge of their own destiny and future.
- Therefore, along with the physical infrastructure, we very consciously work on bringing about a major change in the attitudes, consciousness, dreams and aspirations, the will to overcome obstacles, old habits and forces which divide. Make a genuine difference not only to their way of living, but also to their way of thinking and being.
- The village community is encouraged to fix goals, identify problems, seek solutions, raise resources from within, supplemented with funds and resources from outside. Equality of opportunity for the marginalized sections.
- We bring together as partners—the village community, NGOs, corporate houses and the Government to work in a cohesive manner for optimum use of resources and energies. Look for new and creative ideas so as to develop a sustainable and replicable model.

Integral (Rural) Development—How different is it?

Essentially both are 'rural' but the basic tenet or the bottom line is entirely different. In fact, these are two entirely different paradigms. They can be put across like this.

Integral (Rural) Development	*Integrated (Rural) Development*
• It is human-spirit centred, while not ignoring the need to have the essentials of life including better income for families.	• It has more to do with common facilities and assets plus raising income levels of individuals and families.
• Begin at the bottom and work up to the apex. That is, SARVAM works with the people from the ground up.	• Plan at the top and execute a blueprint down to the grassroots (IRDP model executed in 1970s).
• Work on an individual's (or family's) thinking and being.	• It ignores or is indifferent to a person's thinking and being.
• It works also at the emotional and spiritual self of individuals, while not ignoring their material well-being.	• It works focusing on the essentials of life in materialistic terms.

Integral (Rural) Development	*Integrated (Rural) Development*
• Aims at achieving societal change through raising self-awareness and civic conscience, leading to sustainable rural transformation.	• Aims at achieving economic change, and improving the physical facilities of households.
• Enhancing the monetary income of a person to raise her/him above the Poverty Line threshold is not integral development unless the person has learnt dignity and self-respect as well in the process of earning her/him income.	• Reduction in income poverty levels of the population.
• It is broader in connotation.	• It is narrow in what it intends to integrate or achieve.

Integral Development

To get the meaning of 'integral' right we must, first of all, understand that it subsumes two things here. First, it is about overall development in the routine use of the term meaning all kinds of facilities that improve the standard of living, and ease drudgery in earning one's income. Secondly, it is about civic consciousness, or a transformation in consciousness. It is about a mode of life that points to the path of enhancing the 'quality of life'.

Integral development does not aim at bodily welfare, at the expense of spiritual welfare. This is what we refer to, when we say spirituality or spiritual approach to development, and NOT in the general use of the term in India with a religious reading into it. It is human-soul centred, or human spirit-centred. Modern science and technology, and consumerist culture help conquer the nature to satisfy 'bodily welfare'. This is not sustainable. It cannot lead to sustainable transformation of rural areas. Civic consciousness is about the quality of one's thinking and responsible well-being.

For example, a toilet is an integral part of a house. Minus a toilet a building with one or two living rooms, a prayer room, a kitchen etc. is not called a house, in the true sense. Visiting such a house, everything is seemingly present in abundance. But something significant is missing—the toilet. The occupants say: we defecate in the open. It makes your face shrink. That is because an integral element is missing. You are not able to take it for a complete house because of the absence of a toilet in the house. You are not able to accept that the occupants lead a 'quality life' because of the absence of sanitation culture. It makes you weigh the quality of the person himself/herself and conclude the quality of life they lead is poor.

Physical welfare, sans spiritual welfare is not integral development. Self-awakening, self-respect and dignity are essentials of integral rural development, which SARVAM has tried to create. Integrated rural development is often quantitatively measurable and output oriented; whereas integral development is qualitative, and observable mostly through the quality of human transactions. Thus, SARVAM believes that the shaping of consciousness is the fundamental source of social change, and the nature of social change we are likely to achieve.

The words 'development' and 'transformation' are interchangeably used in this report, although there is a vast difference between these two concepts in development parlance. The development tenets SARVAM aimed at translating on the ground in the service villages are: (i) Social well-being; (ii) Economic well-being; (iii) Spiritual or emotional well-being; and (iv) Political well-being, which eventually should result in integral development or rural transformation taking shape.

The Stakeholders

1. Primary Stakeholders	
1.1 Children	**Interest in Village Development Project**
	Academice ducation, computer education, active play, nutritious food
1.2 Women	Livelihood diversification, nutritional education, revolving fund, useful leisure time
1.3 Vulnerable and marginalized above	Housing renovation, livelihoods, revolving fund, motivation to rise poverty line
1.4 Youth	Multiple developmental activities, sports and games, education, official connections
1.5 Committee members	Local recognition, good governance
1.6 Panchayats	Development beyond the reach of government schemes, good governance, development guidance
2. Secondary Stakeholders	
2.1 Hospitals (SLIMS, JIPMER)	General health care provision, health extension to benefit rural people, rural connections, assistance to the poor (Arvind Eye Hospital, Govt. Hospital etc.)
2.2 Auroville	Overall development
2.3 JCI Metro Pondy	Social responsibility
2.4 Rotary International	Social responsibility
2.5 School Teachers	Improve children's performance in academic activities

2.6 Volunteers	Useful community work, self-satisfaction
2.7 Well-wishers	Useful community work, self-satisfaction
2.8 Chinmaya Mission	Spiritual development
2.9 Azim Premji Foundation	Overall development
2.10 Cadbury	Overall development of villages (women, children, youth, Panchayats through CSR)
2.11 HP	Computer access to rural school children
2.12 US Embassy	English access programme, English for village children
2.13 Lamda Foundation	Women empowerment
2.14 Government (DRDA)	Additional hands for development promotion
2.15 LTFS	Education, Women Empowerment and Digital Financial Literacy
2.16 HDFC	Sanitation and Covid Relief Activities
2.17 TCS	Computer Education
3. Key Stakeholders	
3.1 Children	Education, active play, computers, nutrition
3.2 Women	Livelihoods, revolving fund, useful leisure
3.3 Village Committee	Good governance in practice
3.4 Aravind Eye Hospital	Eye care to the rural poor through outreach
3.5 JCI	Social Responsibility
3.6 Chinmaya Mission	Spiritual development

Ideas for Expansion: The SARVAM village development programme has been initiated and is working as a rural development unit of Sri Aurobindo Society. It is also promoting other supportive institutions for rural transformation to take place, one of which is Sharanam—Centre for Sustainable Rural Transformation. These institutions are being created to serve the purpose of reaching out to other villages and the larger community, expanding SARVAM in practice, gradually to expand the work to more and more villages.

We shall see in the chapters that follow what SARVAM has achieved so far; what are its plans for spreading out; and what is the idea of Sharanam etc.

Chapter 3

Development in Practice

Areas of Intervention

The purpose of this chapter is to give a complete account of activities carried out in Poothurai and Perambai Village Panchayats in Villupuram from 2005 to 2012; and in the subsequent expansion phase beginning from 2012 to 2022. Tracking the development that has taken place in a society is easier than tracking the transformation that has taken place. This is mainly because by nature ***development can be reported in terms of sectors, whereas capturing a transformation process is often complex and overlapping. It shows something on the surface while deep down what is going on could be something different.*** It is often not subject to accurate measurements, thus are beyond easy comprehension. However, proxy measurements and deep context-specific observations and recording are possible.

This observation of comparing the behaviour of the people is best done by someone who has been closely associated with the community in question for quite a reasonable period of time. It might require a kind of anthropological study employing participant-observation methods, and vignettes. It is trying to understand the developmental aspirations of a community—if they are trying to become self-reliant or externally dependent. ***Capturing what is going on deep down in the minds of people, and the way they think and aspire; what they value most; and what they value least. All these are vital in capturing a transformation process.***

This book is an assessment of works carried out almost from the beginning, in constant interaction with the social workers associated with the service villages for quite some years. Therefore, a reasonably good comparison of counter-factuality could be done wherever required. However, this chapter aims at presenting only the activities carried out in plain language—no varnishing, and no embellishments.

As mentioned earlier, the key ingredients of a transformation process are far too strong and complicated to explain than that of a normal sector-specific development process. In order to resolve the problem of overlapping in the transformation process and to enable ease of reading, the presentation made begins with sector-specific development, which in any ways cannot be ignored.

The rural development interventions carried out by SARVAM during the period 2012-2023 in the service villages are in the areas of Education, Health and Sanitation, Rural Livelihoods Promotion, Housing, Support to the marginalized, Digital Literacy, Digital Financial Transactions, Women Development, Youth Development, Media for Social Change, and offering a vast array of software and hardware training programmes of various duration to serve varied purposes. A brief account of each activity and the results achieved are presented below.

Education

Holistic Education: Education is a fundamental area of the Integral Village Development Programme. The first intervention SARVAM made was in Education. Educational intervention starts from pre-school to secondary level, and guidance for higher studies are offered as well. The Programme aims at taking holistic education to the villages, focusing on development of physical, emotional, psychological and spiritual dimensions of the humanself, adapting its delivery to suit rural conditions. A complete change in the attitude of the entire community towards children's education, including by the school authorities, Panchayat leaders and parents, from apathy to active involvement was the primary achievement in the field of education.

The programme was also instrumental in bringing about dramatic improvements in both 'hard infrastructure' and 'soft infrastructure' in the local schools. By hard infrastructure is meant, for example, the school buildings constructed or renovated; and soft infrastructures are aspects such as arts, culture, yoga, development of rural sports and games, organising summer camps etc. It has made the overall school environment more conducive to children's education. A computer centre was set up and the dilapidated school buildings were renovated and many strategies have been adopted to ensure that the children attend school.

In addition to academics, the Village Development Programme maintains a concentrated focus on character and personality building in the process of imparting curricular and physical education to rural children. The aim is to ignite the aspiration for self-development and self-reliance in them. Improving infrastructure, enhancing facilities, creating awareness in the village community, motivating teachers, involving parents, expanding the domains to physical and cultural education and effectively aligning government support are the primary focus of child education. The Village Programme has been able to achieve 100 per cent enrolment of eligible children in primary schools.

English Language Proficiency

The English language course with US Embassy was completed by 450 students in four batches and they gained knowledge. They now feel more confident in their ability to use English and communicate effectively in a variety of contexts.

There were two students who were able to go to USA on a one-month exchange programme and more than 30 students who attended workshops in Pune, Mysore and Chennai, resulting in a significant change in attitude among students and parents. Their narration of their first flight experience goes as an endless Mega serial.

The English knowledge and confidence that the course provides have led to many students enrolling in good colleges, something that did not happen in this village's history before. This has been a major turning point for the village and its people. Better opportunities have opened up for them and their families. Social and economic development in the village has been on the rise ever since.

There is now a great deal of confidence among the rural students from our service villages in participating in the competitions even if the competition is in English, which is an important development. The illiterate parents are very proud of the courage of their children to face the world.

Making Institutions Functional: A village school is an important local institution but what renders an institution vibrant or dormant depends on persons managing these institutions. A school building in Poothurai was found to be dilapidated. Renovating the building required funds for which the school headmaster and Village Panchayat President had to meet and discuss. But these are heads of two different institutions. Ideally speaking they should discuss and sort out issues.

The Panchayat President belonged to the Scheduled Caste, so the headmaster seemed to have felt that it was below his dignity to approach and initiate the talk. The Panchayat President was indifferent to that issue perhaps, because he did not realize he was supposed to be head of the Village Education Committee (VEC) as well, as per the Tamil Nadu Panchayati Raj Act. It was a procedural requirement that any proposal from a village school should go through the Panchayat President. SARVAM staff observed what was going on.

SARVAM, playing the mediator, then arranged for a meeting of the school headmaster and the Village Panchayat President. They found that the Universal Primary Education for all (SSA) Programme had funds for infrastructure building in schools. The application was to go from the school, with the approval of the Panchayat President. The school got a sanction of Rs.10,000 but the amount was found insufficient. Then SARVAM contributed Rs. 30,000. The total amount was spent on renovating the school building. Ultimately, the children benefit. Families benefit.

Bringing two institutions to work for a common cause in a village required a mediator like SARVAM to help sort out the differences. SARVAM played the mediator to resolve issues so that development takes place in the village. When a silence is to be broken someone has to play the mediator.

GOVERNMENT SCHOOLS GET A FACELIFT

The Government of Tamil Nadu, after initiating the Universal Education for All (Sarva Siksha Abhiyan—SSA) has been making attempts to introduce innovative teaching methods in government schools. Yet the ground reality is that enrolment in government schools is low, whereas privately-run schools thrive and flourish all-over the state. There are several reasons for this state of affairs. SARVAM aims at making sure that government schools in SARVAM's area of action get all necessary facilities like adequate buildings, furniture, classrooms, drinking water and sanitation, playground, play materials, educational materials, computers and so on. Moreover, children get introduced to a variety of extra-curricular activities, supplementary coaching in the evenings, and a children's corner to mould the all-round personality of children. It has helped to remove the poor impression the community members had had about government schools. It has also helped to improve the loyalty of government school teachers in these places. The pass percentage in SSLC examination year after year, and the marks students score send across positive messages in favour of enrolling children in government schools. Children who had left for private schools shifted into reverse gear and got readmitted to government schools. This is something extraordinary in Tamil Nadu State, where the general trend is government schools' enrolment gets lower and lower year after year. SARVAM also allows educational loans be taken from their Community Revolving Fund. It gives confidence to the community members to make higher education possible.

Similarly, there were complaints from parents of teachers not being punctual in the school; and the teachers on the other hand accusing parents of being irresponsible about or indifferent to the homework assigned by the teachers. SARVAM arranged for a meeting of the Village Education Committee (VEC), and Parents and Teachers Association (PTA) in the school premises. To the surprise of SARVAM staff, they found the past Panchayat President (who also belonged to the SC community) taking a lead role in organizing the meeting. This tripartite meeting of parents, teachers, and the VEC in the presence of the Panchayat Presidents (the current and the past) served to ventilate the bottled up feelings from all sides. After all of them had aired their views, everybody felt relieved and the differences of opinion subsided. And everyone's consciousness got an

Village Education Committee

SARVAM believes in facilitating the community to take the responsibility to make decisions, and own whatever common assets are built. The decisions made must be through institutions that have local grounding. In each village where SARVAM works, a Village Education Committee (VEC) has been formed. There are also functional Parent-Teacher Associations (PTAs). The presence of these committees is supportive of any development that is planned with regard to the improvement of school education. There is also constant orientation taking place for these committees. The VEC at Poothurai, with the guidance of SARVAM, has been able to move the District Educational Officers to elevate the local Middle School into a High School. They have also mobilized funds from Auroville Action Group to pay the deposit required for elevating the status of the school. The VEC through the initiative of the VP President got additional classrooms constructed with government funds. SARVAM with the cooperation of the PTA is organizing an annual educational tour for school children. These are indications that the VEC can serve as potential local institutions to take over and sustain educational benefits in the event of SARVAM withdrawing.

awakening that they needed to be a little more responsible—as parents and teachers. Bringing local institutions to play their role effectively, and creating an awakening in their consciousness that before pointing the finger at others one needs to look inward into oneself. SARVAM was needed to bring into play such a consciousness awakening for the benefit of the children.

RESULTS

1000 preschool children; 1000 students at primary and secondary level; and 500 students at high school level, 500 students from higher secondary level, 200 students from college level benefit from the education programmes of SARVAM.

1500 students have been assisted with educational scholarships and educational loans; 1000 students have learnt to use computers; and 2000 students use the children's corner for innovative learning.

Childcare Centres: In some places like Manaveli hamlet, there were complaints from parents that the staff in-charge of a Childcare Centre was handling the children poorly. Upon discussion the teacher admitted she found it difficult to handle all the children single-handedly, without any support or assistance. SARVAM, with the assistance of Auroville, got the services of a volunteer to assist in the childcare centre. The centre started performing to the satisfaction of the parents, and the teacher also felt she had been heard and supported.

As a result of SARVAM's efforts, currently all the children in the hamlets, covered by the Programme, in the age group of 2 to 5 years are attending preschool. Eight preschools have been renovated with the assistance of SARVAM. Through regular awareness and motivational initiatives, the Village Programme has been able to invoke an active interest in mothers of the village towards their children's education, health, hygiene and well-being. Volunteers and non-governmental organizations in the field of child education regularly visit the preschool and conduct fun classes for the children and their mothers. Outings and day tours are

VAZHAPATTAMPALAYAM CHILDCARE CENTRE

A Childcare Centre (also known as 'play school'/'preschool'/'anganwadi' for children between 3–5 years of age) at Vazhapattampalayam in Perambai Village Panchayat serves as a model childcare centre for 35 preschools in Villupuram district, Tamil Nadu. It was set up in 1982 with minimal facilities. It did not even have a building to house the children and was functioning in a thatched hut. A site survey was made by the Village Administrative Officer (VAO) in 1990 to construct a building for the preschool and which materialized almost after a decade. The preschool got a building in the year 2000 but with an asbestos sheet roof. One Ms. Saraswathipai (now 50 years old) serves as teacher. She is assisted by a worker who cooks and runs errands. SARVAM started working in Perambai Panchayat in 2006 and during a discussion with Ms. Saraswathipai she mentioned that the asbestos sheet roof was a matter of concern and also a lack of play materials and toys for the children. SARVAM, recognising the sincerity of the teacher, found the funds to replace the asbestos sheet with a reinforced concrete roof and to provide play materials and toys for the children.

Volunteers who visited SARVAM works in Perambai (especially Ms. Alisa and Mr. Shankar) spent time doing play-way learning techniques with the children at the childcare centre. Volunteers with the help of local youth cleared the bushes around the preschool and introduced outdoor games too. Parents' interest in sending children to that childcare centre improved.

The centre also started orientating parents on child care, and nutrition related aspects. The school became well-liked in the locality. Admission and attendance became matchless compared to other ones in the neighbourhood.

The Government Department of Women and Child Development uses this centre as a model for training teachers to be employed in Childcare Centres. The contributions of SARVAM and the personal interest shown by the teacher [Ms Saraswathipai] must be attributed for the success of this preschool in Perambai. Other preschools in SARVAM's working areas (Manaveli, Poothurai, Poothurai colony) have also been assisted in various ways, including setting up of grounds for outdoor games, supplying toys and educational materials, construction of toilets, and volunteer support.

arranged for the schoolchildren, where their mothers are involved, both as organizers as well as participants in the Programme.

Supplementary Coaching: In order to improve the performance of secondary school students in Poothurai village SARVAM had arranged supplementary education programmes between 4.00-5.00 pm in the school. Thus, SARVAM has appropriately intervened wherever required—be it childcare centre, or primary school or secondary school winning the confidence of the parents as well as the local institutions. Making the local institutions functional is an important task that SARVAM has taken up. The Programme identifies marginalized and needy students and provides academic, social and material support to them so that they can overcome any adverse economic or family circumstances and continue their education. The Programme provides financial support in the form of scholarships and loans to poor, deserving students and also helps in conducting evening coaching classes. The headmasters of schools in SARVAM's operational area report of improved performance of the children and this is reflected in the results of the schools' final examinations as well.

Children's Corner: SARVAM has implemented a unique concept of weekly informal sessions for children—the Children's Corner—

where they get the freedom and opportunity to cultivate their interests in dancing, singing, sports, art, handicrafts, drama etc. These Children's Corner, started in 2007, provide the right environment for children to grow, communicate and develop into confident individuals.

SARVAM's Key Differentiator is the integrated nature of community development where both tangible aspects like housing and education co-exist with intangible aspects like character building and integrity.

Nearly 250 children, between the age of 5-15, attend these 7 centres. These camps, with the focus on a specific curriculum, are

CHILDREN'S CORNER

Children's Corner could be termed a unique or innovative programme of SARVAM. It aims at a multidimensional personality development of rural children. Children in Poothurai and Perambai villages come from varied backgrounds with different types of family pressures—some are children of single parent, some have drunkard fathers, or widowed mothers struggling to send their children to school and so on. Building confidence in such children through activities that are multi-skill oriented is the prime task of Children's Corner. It moulds the overall personality of children with the idea of preparing them to face the challenges that may await them.

Children's Corner arranges for a range of extra-curricular activities such as indoor games, folk-dance, songs, meditation, creative arts, communication skills, pencil drawing and colouring, academic counselling and guidance. Parents derive great pleasure watching their children perform dances, play chess, participate in cricket, do pencil sketches and so on. SARVAM conducts annual competitions during summer camps and distributes prizes. It is motivating and keeps the interest of children alive and active. The venue used for supplementary evening classes/additional coaching classes serve as centres for these Children's Corner too.

opportunities where children can learn and enhance their potential. The camp expenses are undertaken by the people of the villages, while the volunteers generally provide the supplies and materials. There is a lot of involvement from the village community coming together in a joyous spirit of self-reliance in the activities of these Children's Corner.

Summer Camps: Summer camps are an extension of the Children's Corner, where the concept of holistic development of children is the core theme. This is being held year after year since the beginning of SARVAM's Village Programme. The various curricula adopted in the summer camps where children participate in large numbers include vocal and instrumental music, martial arts, science and technology, computers and multimedia, art and craft. The camps also include unique workshops

HOW A SUMMER CAMP FUNCTIONS

A summer camp is usually held for 3 to 4 weeks. It starts from 6.30 am to 7 pm. The days are packed with nearly 35 to 40 fun-filled, yet educative sessions for all age groups of the participating children. It is usually planned for children in the age group of 6 to 17, with activities such as learning new skills, character-and-discipline-building exercises, art forms, sports and games, health check-ups, outdoor trips, spiritual knowledge, handicrafts, stimulating and intellectual games and other such extracurricular activities. There are also activities such as Bharatnatyam, folk dances and other semi-classical dance forms; playing musical instruments, vocal music, martial arts, sketching, drawing and painting, performing a puppet show, yoga and other exercises, computer games, story-telling, beadwork and stitching, organized and spontaneous sporting activities and so on. Doctors from various renowned hospitals of Pondicherry visit the camp for eye and dental check-up of children. The children are always engaged and kept smiling or laughing. Activities are planned and carried out with the fact in mind that the attention span of children is less if children are not completely

(*Contd.*)

involved in the activity. Besides the various planned activities the children get juice/fruits/snacks twice a day, in addition to a nutritious mid-day meal.

I am very grateful to SARVAM for sending my daughter to an All India level workshop at Mysore without any expense. It was a great pleasure to have my daughter receive a cash prize of 20,000 for her best performance at the all-India level participation on community service work at Mysore. As a result of her participation in SARVAM's weekend classes from childhood, she gained a lot of knowledge in a variety of fields.

She travelled to Mysore for the first time on a flight, and as her illiterate father, I could not explain the feelings. Now she is very confident in her future life. I am thanking SARVAM and asking them to help many more underprivileged rural students like my daughter.

conducted by experts on building character, integrity, confidence, leadership attitudes and entrepreneurial skills, on controlling emotions and nurturing values. The highly motivated children take responsibility for the daily chores of the camp with exemplary ownership and collective pride. Over the years it has become something the children enthusiastically look forward to after schools close for summer vacation so they can enjoy the fun of the various activities planned for them during the camp. The camps, which are usually held for almost 3 weeks, require detailed planning much in advance.

Project Ringtone: A unique initiative, in partnership with Hewlett-Packard, the Project Ringtone helps in cultivating computer awareness and expertise among the village students to enable them to design and implement its use in the rural context and setting. Training is given to children in the age group of 10–16 years primarily on two applications — 'Movie Soup' helps them to learn animation and visualize and narrate a story through it

while 'Scratch' helps them develop their analytical and mathematical skills while learning the basics of programming. Being able to work with computers demystifies the technology-fear, and it builds confidence that they too can work with computers.

> Children draw a mind-map of some stories and design animation pictures using software such as 'movie Soup' or 'scratch'. Rural school children demonstrate their ease in using computers, and we find it reflects in their academic performance as well.

Health Interventions

Primary health care is another integral aspect of rural development. The Government sub-health centre in Poothurai which had gone defunct and dilapidated was renovated and made functional to cater to the basic health needs of the villagers. A nurse and some paramedics were appointed for the clinic. A tie-up was made with Sri Lakshmi Narayana Institution of Medical Science and Hospital (SLIMS) so that patients with more serious ailments would be taken there and treated on a regular basis. After a health survey, SARVAM along with Lakshmi Narayana Hospital staff issued health cards with all necessary details for every family in the village. People were made aware of government programmes, which provide health insurance to the people. SARVAM in collaboration with premier medical institutes in Puducherry such as the Pondicherry Institute of Medical Sciences (PIMS), JIPMER and the Aravind Eye Hospital have been organizing other health programmes such as dental camps, eye treatments and surgeries, immunization camps for children and general health check up of expecting women are being conducted on a regular basis.

HEALTH CARE NETWORK OF SARVAM

Sri Aurobindo Society is the first reference for SARVAM. This helps maintain good relationship with a network of health care institutions. They include: Aravind Eye Hospital, Pondicherry, Pondicherry Institute of Medical Sciences (PIMS), JIPMER, Pondicherry, SLIMS. There are periodical health camps conducted on general health, eye care, dental care, care of the aged, vaccination for children, de-worming, supply of iron tablets for anaemic women and so on. SARVAM organizes village level camps as well as arranges for the transport of people/patients, for medical follow-up and advice. In most cases it is done free of cost. There is also a health insurance policy of a private Insurance Company (Star) with which SARVAM has encouraged the people to become policy holders.

Some of the highlights of this Programme are as follows:

- Periodical health camps in collaboration with JIPMER, PIMS and SLIMS continue to be organized. A series of health checks for school children has been initiated with the necessary follow-up interventions.
- Another successful initiative of the Village Programme has been the commencement of a SLIMS bus service, which has been picking up patients from these adopted villages, every month as scheduled, for general check-ups and treatment, eliminating the distance between patients and the medical help for them.
- One Dr. Tamilarasi from the Government Maternity Hospital in Puducherry has started a monthly session with the women, where she talks about general health care, hygiene, maternal care etc.

INTEREST-FREE LOAN FOR MEDICAL EXPENDITURE

Ms. Suguna (50), Perambai: Ms. Suguna used to suffer from severe stomach pain quite often. She consulted the doctors at Manakula Vinayakar Medical College Hospital. They advised her to undergo a minor surgical operation that might cost Rs.14,000. She decided to put up with the pain after hearing how much it would cost to undergo the minor surgical operation. She continued to suffer from pain but did not have the courage to borrow from any source because of the fear of the high rate of interest charged on loans taken from private sources. Obviously, no bank would be willing to lend money for medical expenses. The SARVAM field team came to know of the plight of Suguna during a women's group meeting. SARVAM gave her an amount as an interest-free loan. She was to repay it in easy instalments. She underwent the operation, and has since repaid the loan too. She is thankful to SARVAM for the timely help.

VISION REGAINED

Ganesan (62), Poothurai: I lost my vision when I was about 54-55 years old. I used to walk holding someone's hand, often one of my grandchildren's. I lost all hope in life, and thought I would never see the world again. In an accidental meeting with SARVAM staff I was told, 'At Aravind Hospital in Pondicherry it is possible to go for an eye surgery'. In one of the eye camps organized by SARVAM, I got to know from an ophthalmologist that my problem could not be cured through a cataract operation but that I required eye transplantation. They asked me to wait and have faith in God. Like they say, 'every sincere prayer is answered', and I got an eye transplant. Now I keep SARVAM staff and the Aravind Eye Hospital doctors in my prayers.

RESULTS

So far SARVAM constructed 400 individual household toilets jointly with Government. Conducted many awareness programmes to the community people and students. Now all houses having household toilets. Awareness programmes on waste management to the community and students conducted. More than 200 nutri-gardens promoted with SARVAM's Assistance. Nutri-gardens are being raised and providing at least 200 households with vegetables.

Sanitation and Safe Water Supply

The individual household toilets construction programme has been carried out with community participation. Sixty household toilets have been constructed during the first phase. The popular Sulabh model toilets, approved by WHO and UNICEF, is being used as an appropriate design for rural areas. Safe drinking water has also been arranged with financial contribution shared by the community and government. The initiatives to create awareness about sanitation and toilet culture, and the Programme's toilet construction programmes have, in these few years, resulted in marked improvement in the overall environment and health conditions in the villages. Most households now have toilet facilities, whereas at the time of commencement of SARVAM's village work, hardly one in a hundred houses had toilets. Of late, more and more households are taking up the construction of toilets with government assistance. They are efficiently managing the construction by following the Village Programme's model—'SARVAM model'— of

SANITATION IMPROVEMENT

Twelve-year-old Arun Kumar, forced his illiterate parents to make individual household toilet for their house. For his studies, he said that if the toilet wasn't built he would go to his grandparents' house. His parents were initially reluctant, but Arun's insistence and his promise to clean the toilets himself everyday led them to agree. He inspired many other families in his village to build toilets and improved the overall health and sanitation of his community.

As a result of SARVAM's awareness programme and financial assistance, not only Arun, but many of the students convinced their parents to construct toilets in their houses. They also insisted on cleanliness. This improved the overall health of the village and reduced water-borne diseases. This in turn led to improved school attendance and better academic performance among the students. The village also saw a decrease in the number of cases of diarrhoea and other water-borne diseases. The success of this programme also inspired other villages to start similar programmes.

Additionally, the panchayat has a clean green village plan and youth have started giving awareness on plastics and garbage to the community. The panchayat has implemented a biodegradable waste management system, and the local youth have been actively involved in educating people in the community about the importance of proper waste management. This has led to a significant reduction in plastic and other forms of waste in the villages.

the previous years.

Villagers tend to spend in thousands for temple festivals. But they do not understand the need to contribute towards the creation or maintenance of common facilities in the village—be it water supply system, drainage, or street lights. Getting their mindset changed in favour of owning common assets could be an ultimate test of community ownership.

Housing

Housing is found to be one of the most successful initiatives of the Integral Village Development Programme. Owning a house is the dream of almost every Indian family. This is also one of the areas where the housing scheme of the government could be made use of for the benefit of deserving members of the community. Prior to the initiation of this project, most houses in this area were in dilapidated, decrepit conditions, leaving people exposed to the rigours of weather and other natural calamities. The health of people was also at stake with non-existent or poor roofing over their heads.

The Village Programme initially helped in constructing and renovating houses for the needy. The funds the Village Programme provided for the construction of houses were all in the form of loans and not grants, in line with the Trust's aim to make the villagers self-reliant. Most of the loans have been recovered. In fact about 90 per cent recovery rate has been achieved, which was due to the financial responsibility, ownership, and pride factor felt by the people of the villages.

The Village Programme's volunteers also realized that though there were a number of government programmes and schemes for the poor to apply and receive loans for housing and other needs, most of the rural population was unaware of these programmes. This led to these funds being either underused or misused. When the Village Programme started to educate the local citizenry, it brought in a radical change in the hitherto speculative process of selection of the beneficiaries for the government housing schemes. The selection process is now equitable, more transparent, offering the last man first.

Inspired by the movement, many of the people of the village have also taken up the initiative to improve their houses by constructing with better, stronger materials, applying for loans to other agencies and government organizations for the same. Village Housing Committees (VECs) were formed by the Village Programme to identify beneficiaries, help in the construction, and monitor progress of on-going construction projects.

The housing initiative has demonstrated a sea-change in the attitude of the people of the village towards self-reliance and also brought in

HOUSING THE POOR

V.S. Murugan (34), Manaveli: Murugan lived with his wife, three children and aged parents in Manaveli. His was a very much dilapidated house. He had a heavy vehicle driving licence and planned to buy a mini-van for passenger transport, which he thought would solve all his financial difficulties. To acquire the full amount required to buy the vehicle, he sold a piece of land also and became a vehicle owner. Contrary to his planning, he incurred heavy loss as he was unable to manage the passenger transport and had to sell the vehicle. Unfortunately at the same time his hut caught fire. House gone, vehicle gone, land gone, he felt drained of all hopes and often entertained suicidal thoughts.

It was at that time the local Housing Committee (Poothurai) included his name in the list of poorest of the poor deserving assistance for constructing a house. The hope that he was going to get a new house with RCC roofing, gave him the energy to carry on life with a positive outlook. The SARVAM team counselled him that losing hope was not going to take him anywhere. He somehow mobilized the financial contribution he had to make and got the house sanctioned and constructed it with the support of his family members. He is now the proud owner of a small but good house. His wife has become a member of the local women's group that is involved in thrift and credit activities. The family members, especially his aged parents, are regular attendees at the health camps organized by SARVAM. Murugan now earns his living by driving and is full of confidence in his mind, and a lot of gratitude for the people of SARVAM who lent a helping hand at a time when he felt completely broken, and thought he had reached the end of his life. Thus he considers SARVAM as a real saviour.

awareness of rights and a sense of dignity in the families staying in the newly constructed or renovated and secure houses. We look back with satisfaction that the importance and visibility given to the housing programme during the previous years has brought about a social and communal change in the families and households. Overall, health and education have improved. People are now more knowledgeable and demanding of their rights *vis-à-vis* the government schemes and programmes specifically initiated for them. The aspiration to own a house and to take the effort of saving money for it by working harder is increasing, thus, leading to improved earnings and saving habits also.

Being a fund-intensive activity, the Village Programme has discontinued the construction of new houses. It is now facilitating people to effectively utilize the government housing schemes (PMAY-G) by following the housing model created in the previous years. However, it continues to help families in distress to renovate their houses. Whenever required, the Village Programme continues to administer and guide the construction of houses and help in the selection of beneficiaries for government schemes.

PANJALAI'S FAMILY GETS A NEW LEASE OF LIFE

Panjalai (38), Manaveli: Panjalai, whose husband is a wood cutter, is an active woman. They are a family of seven, with four sons and one daughter. The family was mired in poverty because of the drinking habit of the husband. The eldest daughter dropped out after she failed in her secondary education. They were living in a house that was a dilapidated hut. Life was very difficult especially during rainy seasons. Panjalai joined the Women's Group with the hope of improving these conditions. When SARVAM started their programme for improving the housing condition of the poorest of the poor in Manaveli village, the responsibility of selecting beneficiaries was entrusted to a locally constituted Housing Committee. To her luck, Panjalai was selected as a beneficiary. She got a new house with a concrete roof in place of the hut she was living in. She borrowed from the revolving fund of the local women's group in order to make the financial contribution for the house construction.

SARVAM also provided financial assistance of up to Rs. 2,000 for her to take up vegetable vending in Puducherry. She also borrowed from the revolving fund to buy a bicycle for her son to go to school which is five kilometres away. By doing this she prevented her son from dropping out of school. Experiencing the development that is taking place in their family, her husband has given up drinking and now contributes to the family income. Her life has taken many positive turns since her association with SARVAM—she got a good house constructed, her son continues his education, she herself is earning a daily income through vegetable vending, and her school drop-out daughter is also employed in a private firm. Above all, she is full of confidence about life and never turns to moneylenders for relief from her financial difficulties.

RESULTS

The Village Development Project has helped renovate 110 houses and construct 70 new concrete houses. The project also influenced the Government Housing Programme to be implemented in an equitable and fair way. The Housing Project has helped to not only protect them from the rigours of weather and other natural calamities, but also to give them a sense of dignity and self-worth.

Employment and Livelihood

This programme was initiated as a multi-dimensional approach to address the issues of unemployment and underemployment in the community; expand the potential for agriculture and allied activities; promotion of micro enterprises; development and upgrading of skills; adapt to local industries; promote links with neighbouring manufacturing industries by facilitating outsourcing of ancillary processes to the villages. The Village Development Programme has encouraged individuals to be self-employed and self-reliant by providing a variety of alternative rural livelihood options such as dairy units, tailoring, vegetable vending, carpentry etc. The Project has been successful in inspiring local people to take up such activities.

In order to generate employment in the village, a tie-up with leather product manufacturing units in Pondicherry was established to outsource components to women in the village. They were provided with the necessary training and equipment. It benefited 40 women who earned a minimum of Rs. 50 a day. But later SARVAM found

that the leather-related work did not interest the women and as they stopped reporting for work one by one, it had to be closed down. They found more interest in engaging themselves in farm-related work, or work that involved using tools such as spades, crow-bars etc. Later they moved on to work for the MG National Rural Employment Guarantee Scheme (MGNREGS), where they are assured of 100 days employment a year. This also helps them get used to handling bank transactions as their wages are credited into a bank account. Earnings from the MGNREG Programme help them repay the SHG loans they took for renovation of their house or for other needs.

Setting up of the Dairy Group: The idea and the proposal of setting up a dairy group originated from the village women themselves and SARVAM worked with them to make it a reality. Seventy five interested and deserving women from the villages, who were already familiar with tending cows were selected for the programme. They were given adequate training in cattle-rearing, fodder and azolla cultivation by resource personnel from M.S. Swaminathan Research Foundation and Krishi Vigyan Kendra. To initiate the programme, 75 cows were procured at a cost of Rs. 12,000 each, which SARVAM advanced as a loan to each of the women.

A veterinarian and a volunteer from PONLAIT (the dairy cooperative of the Pondicherry government) assisted in ensuring the selection of healthy cows. Some of these women cultivated fodder and azolla themselves and supplied it to the other women also. SARVAM arranged a marketing tie-up with PONLAIT to sell 8 to 10 litres of milk per day. The collection of milk and its transportation to the PONLAIT procurement centres was arranged by the women themselves. From the first month onwards, each woman was able to take home an amount of Rs. 1000 to Rs. 1500 per month. Additional income was derived from the sale of cow dung as manure. This has helped to increase the nutritional content of the daily food of community members, particularly children, adding to their calcium and protein intake. This project has proved to be highly successful and inspirational.

The application of the dairy model to other economic activities such as goat rearing, poultry, bee-keeping, fish culture etc. proved to be equally successful, establishing many flourishing and enterprising entrepreneurs in the community. SARVAM provided the expertise—by inviting government and private individuals and organizations working in each of these areas—and financial help for all these businesses.

We sell milk for a good price through PONLAIT cooperative. We get access to our own savings and it keeps us away from moneylenders for Diwali expenses. Otherwise, festivities were for moneylenders to celebrate a good business, say the villagers.

Old women and widows, abandoned by their family members and who cannot be employed for physical labour, were assisted by SARVAM in procuring goats for rearing. Micro enterprises such as equipment hiring, photo studio, construction equipment hiring, photocopying etc. have also been promoted. A community revolving fund of Rs. 2,00,000 has enhanced the money circulation in the village. It serves to effectively keep the community away from moneylenders by catering to the small investment needs of the community members. People in dire need and

MILKING DEVELOPMENT

Gunasundari (46), Perambai: Ms Chitra, team member from SARVAM has a tendency to say frequently 'The Divine, have faith in the Divine power and things will fall in place etc.' I got a cow as a livelihood loan from the Village Development programme. It gave me hope of earning a means of income for my family. As months went by I found myself owning 6 cows. I earn Rs. 22 per litre of milk for the milk I supply to the Pondicherry Milk Cooperative. I started this as a livelihood venture, now I am almost an entrepreneur. I must really thank the Divine for the person who handed the first cow to me, and for making me and my family what we are today.

FODDER DEVELOPMENT

Whenever discussions about livelihood diversification and income augmentation cropped up, one constant livelihood venture that came up for discussion was 'milk animal rearing'. When demand for milk cows arose from people of Poothurai and Perambai, one related question that came along was: where to get 'fodder for the cows'? SARVAM approached the Krishi Vigyan Kendra (KVK). They offered fodder stems under their agricultural extension programme. One Mr. Manchini (63) took up the cultivation of this fodder and started selling it locally at Rs. 20 a bundle. He could make several harvests in a year. The villagers who got cows purchased fodder from his farm. Cultivating fodder helped improve his income and he was able to repay the initial loan he had got from SARVAM. Of late, witnessing the profits in fodder cultivation, a few others have also started cultivating fodder.

LIVELIHOOD

Dhakshinamoorthy (60), Poothurai colony: Dhakshinamoorthy is a typical example of living on the edge of poverty. Both his son and daughter are married and Dhakshinamoorthy lives with his wife. He was a fish vendor but age has started telling upon him, yet, he has to make a living. He obtained a loan of Rs. 3000 from SARVAM's revolving fund and restarted his fish-for-sale business on his bicycle. He is earning a profit of not less than Rs. 500 a week, and their life goes on without much difficulty now. He is thankful to SARVAM, for otherwise, he would have fallen into the debt trap of private moneylenders.

distress were not falling prey to usurious and unscrupulous moneylenders anymore.

People are poor, not because they are lazy or they do not have developmental aspirations. But because the livelihood skills they have acquired over the years provide them with very limited choice of occupation. They stretch out and walk successfully when they get

a helping hand, or when they have their capacity enhanced through exposure, information empowerment or through capacity building training programmes.

RESULTS

About 1000 families have benefited through the various livelihood activities initiated. 2000 members of the community have used the revolving fund for various productive purposes. At least 300 of them could be categorized as poorest of the poor. The revolving fund for the community ranges between Rs. 1 lakh to Rs. 2 lakh at any given point of time. This community revolving fund has helped reduce dependency on moneylenders; 5000 women and men have been trained in various aspects of running small business; and the culture of thrift, savings and banking has come about among the villagers.

2,00,000 people were trained in digital financial literacy and 1,00,000 people given awareness on government entitlements. 2,00,000 people given Covid awareness and Vaccination awareness. 30,000 families have got food kit during Covid pandemic that caused havoc to lives and livelihoods.

Women's Development

SARVAM has had an array of programmes that aimed at women's development. These programmes were decided by the local women themselves. This is one advantage of working on a small scale and in a

participatory mode. It enables things to fall in place very relevantly depending on the need. Such initiatives have a tendency to sustain, more so when it is individually managed or family managed. The desilting of a water tank undertaken in the year 2005 was perhaps one of the first interventions of SARVAM in women's employment. It was also considered unique in the region, in the sense that it was led, implemented, supervised and monitored by an all women team. From book-keeping to reporting in accordance to government procedures, everything was done by the women from the local community.

SOCIETAL CHANGE TOWARDS WOMEN

It is one of the miserable aspects of customs and beliefs in Tamil Nadu villages that one should not face up to a widow when one is setting out for work or for something auspicious. Thus widows in Poothurai village used to be confined to their kitchens. The Village Development Project brought women out of their kitchens with varied activities—from savings and credit to livelihoods and pleasure trips to visit tourist-spots. Women do not like being shut behind their kitchen door any more. They are mobile; they participate in augmenting family income; and in common developmental works. When the idea of community pongal was proposed, the villagers got together forgetting their caste differences and made it a grand celebration. This is a significant milestone in the works of SARVAM.

Slowly, women who were uninterested as well as those whose husbands did not like their participating in SARVAM Village Development activities started participating in large numbers.

Now in 2023 SARVAM is a full-fledged village level movement of women, children, and the youth.

Youth Development

Involvement of youth in social development activities is something unique that not many development interventions attempt to take up. SARVAM has successfully channelized the energy of the village youth in planting tree saplings, conducting supplementary tuition classes for school children, maintaining the local library and so on. Some of these youth who had the habit of taking alcohol are now reformed, and conduct games and plays in the evenings. They have started supporting SARVAM's activities, and act as the local coordinators in their implementation.

The village youth could be potential local coordinates to take over in the event of SARVAM withdrawing from these villages. The training they have had, the trust they have earned, and the good relations they enjoy with the SARVAM field team have made them develop a feeling of being part of SARVAM's activities in the two villages. Their positive energy has been channelized into the development programmes for the common good of the local community. As far as the work in the villages is concerned, the local coordinators play the main role. There are over 20 local coordinators (volunteers) working with the Village Development Project.

> We were a bunch of noisy youth at gram sabha meetings. We were nothing more than members of a 'directionless street gang'. But sarvam nurtured us to become members of a 'constructive youth group'. After marriage now, in order to fulfil her desire, I am sending my wife to do her B.Ed.

SARVAM has caused a remarkable change in the attitude of the youth. It has infused a positive energy with significant contributions to self-development. Their active participation in voluntary activities inspires and generates a sense of purpose. They organize and manage the village journal.

YOUTH DEVELOPMENT

The engagement with children and women paved the way for the youth also to get an entry into the development activities of SARVAM. SARVAM was thinking of introducing skills development activities but it found that the youth were interested in sports and games more than enhancing their skills. Things not in the priority of people generally, do not succeed. Therefore, SARVAM went on to support the sports and games activities of the youth, which was their priority. The youth contributed Rs. 5,000 in cash, and SARVAM came up with up to rupees one lakh. The money was used to buy sports articles. The youth then volunteered to clean up the village common grounds and started playing games like volley ball, cricket etc. They also conducted friendly matches and tournaments.

The support SARVAM extended, paying heed to their request made the youth respond to the call of SARVAM when SARVAM suggested using the Community Fund for livelihood activities. Some youth started using the Community Fund to take up livelihood ventures. Then the demand for skill development training started cropping up, and which SARVAM supported. SARVAM supported the development of skills like tailoring, masonry, four-wheeler driving and so on. Some even went on to continue studies that they had discontinued. Some educated youth volunteered to manage the supplementary education classes (tuition centres) that SARVAM initiated. These young people have come to realize the strength of being a member of an organized group; the value of time; and the need for skills development training. The institutional support and guidance rendered by SARVAM, and the connections that SARVAM has enabled them to establish have given them life-changing potentials.

YOUTH GET THEIR VALUES RIGHT

In Villupuram district, where most of SARVAM villages are located, there are more SC youth than others. Their numerical strength gave them a feeling that they were socially strong. Being 'socially strong' meant to them: You walk holding your head up, you don't have to weigh up the strength of your character. They were unorganized gangs of youth, no one belonged to any organized youth club that could get recognition from institutions such as Nehru Yuva Kendra (NYK) or banks. 'Walk the streets and talk trash' was their unwritten principle. As is the nature of things among them, they started enquiring what SARVAM was doing with the children and women. A process of self-reflection started, reflections which led to clarifications, and thence to new strategies for SARVAM to work with them. SARVAM started roping them in one by one as local organizers of various programmes. The involvement of the local youth groups as organizers of the summer camps deserve mention. The change brought about in the mindset of the local youth was through the programmes causing a battle within their inner-self and not merely through their involvement in a series of social, economic and developmental strategies. Now they have become equally active and participatory in the field activities of SARVAM.

IS GIVING WAY GIVING IN?

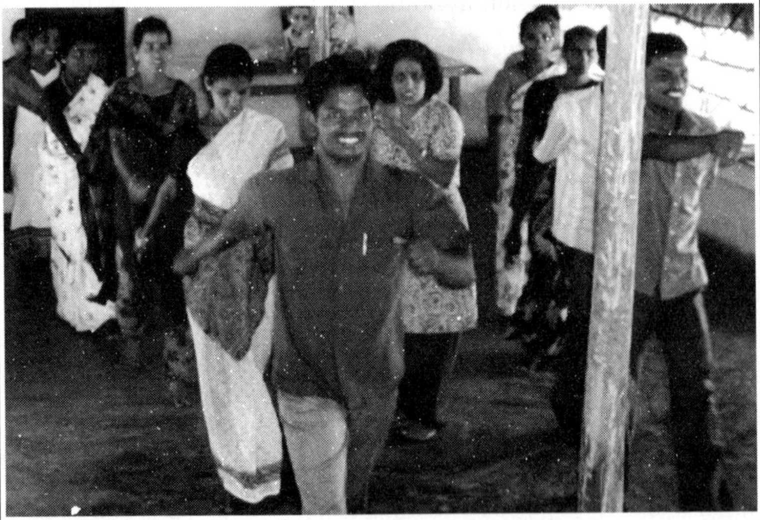

Sasikumar (27) a local youth narrated (to Ms Susan Georgie, CSR Manager of Cadbury), the kind of life the youth led in Poothurai before SARVAM's intervention.

'It had never entered our mind to think beyond the moment we were living. We have been meaninglessly noisy in Gram Sabha and in SARVAM village level meetings, for reasons we never analyzed.

We mistook 'being rude' for 'being bold'.

We mistook 'negativity' for being 'inquisitive'.

We mistook 'distrust' as a means for 'demonstrating self-respect'.

We mistook 'indifference' for 'dignity'.

We mistook 'gang' for 'group'.

We mistook 'giving way' to someone as 'giving in'.

Our gradual association with the Village Development Programme made us realize that giving way is not giving in, rather it is a demonstration of respect for each other; and that it has tremendous potential for connecting two individuals.

We understood 'making a difference matters' rather than being indifferent. We understood the danger of having an 'indifferent mindset'.

SARVAM gave us the ability to expand our vision beyond the conventional boundaries that a naked eye could take notice of.

Community Revolving Fund

The purpose of this fund is to ensure that the rural poor do not approach the moneylenders (or non-institutional sources of finance) for their small credit needs or in times of distress. The usual approach NGOs adopt is to lend micro loans to members of SHGs. But SARVAM's strategy is that any poor should be helped irrespective of whether they are a member or not of an SHG. Initially it was given as interest-free loans. Later on, when the community members started saving and lending from among themselves, they started charging a nominal rate of interest. SARVAM's was just one of those in the whole pool that was available for use as a revolving fund. The surplus earned was divided among the members, and SARVAM's share remained as a common good fund.

COMMUNITY REVOLVING FUND

Sengeniammal (44): Having my 4 children attend higher education is impossible without this SARVAM's revolving fund, and being from a lower class community, higher education is only a dream for us. The revolving fund helped to make sure my children have the best opportunity to succeed and break the cycle of poverty. I'm thankful for resources like this revolving fund that can help make this dream possible. It will give my children the chance to pursue a better future.

This community revolving fund has provided many benefits not only to me, but also to others in my village for various needs. The fund has allowed us to be able to access capital for our livelihood and other needs more quickly and easily than ever before. It has also created a

(*Contd*)

sense of unity and collaboration among us, as we are all helping each other to succeed. This has been a tremendous blessing for all of us.

Community revolving fund that plays an important role among the community in terms of housing, education, livelihood, family functions, and health care. The fund is managed by the community and is available to any member who needs it. Funds are distributed to members on a need-basis, ensuring that everyone in the community has access to the resources they need. The fund is an essential part of the community and helps to ensure its sustainability.

Digital Sakhis Programme

The Digital Sakhi programme has been able to convince, persuade and influence the women entrepreneurs and rural households to use digital banking/digital financial transactions. The DS Programme has demonstrated the facility of online portals of the government to avail various schemes of the government and entitlements of the poor. This requires *continuous engagement for the benefits to sustain.* Financial inclusion is a transformative process. The DS has set the process in motion. SARVAM, along with LTFS, has found ways to sustain the momentum created.

The DS Programme has introduced the habit of thrift and savings. It has initiated many to go for various types of insurance facilities as a way of developing resilience and mitigating risk. This is most likely to go on for ever, which is going to be a business opportunity for the Digital *Seva Kendras* started by some of the DS. The DS Programme has made ordinary women in villages to be recognised as Digital Sakhis. The Digital Sakhis have to be encouraged on the importance of continuous learning, through self-learning.

The improved level of self-confidence, and the recognition of most of the DS and some of the trained women entrepreneurs get at their home front is an achievement in terms of women empowerment, which will go a long way. It's there to stay with them, and take them forward in their journey of life.

The linkage women entrepreneurs have developed with local banks, and the familiarity and regularity in financial transactions—be it for savings, insurance and loans—is most likely to continue. The SARVAM needs to engage them through involving in regular training programmes and capacity building. There was a quick survey conducted in order to know how Digital Sakhi's Programme benefited— (i) the woman trained as Digital Sakhis; (ii) the Entrepreneurs who undertook using the digital mode of financial transactions; and (iii) the community. The results are presented below in three distinct parts.

Part-1: Digital Sakhbis

All the Digital Sakhis interviewed (82 of them) report that their current profession is serving as Digital Sakhis (DS), which indicates the pride they adore to the job they are involved in. This is despite the fact that the primary income generating occupations of the households that DS come from are: (a) either agriculture, or (b) construction related. Some have private jobs, or run grocery and vegetable shops.

Income-Expenditure-Savings: The total monthly savings as reported by most DS (72/82) ranges from Rs. 1,000-2,000. Everyone reported that depending on income, they plan their expenditure and savings. Although everyone reported that they plan their household expenditure, and keep expenses under control, over 92 per cent of them report to have borrowed from SHGs, banks or from MFIs. There are a few who have borrowed from moneylenders also.

Loan Availed: Personal Loan and Education loan top the type of loans obtained by DS families, followed by

Prema, Poothurai, 38 years

I am a mother of two children who live in a hut house that leaks during the rain. Often during such days, I am reminded of the night when roof of this hut fell down on my husband sleeping in the corner of room. The next day I found myself not only as a widow, but an alone woman without any support to raise my family with two adolescent children. Three months prior SARVAM asked me to open a bank account. Initially, I was hesitant but they convinced me about its benefits like government insurance schemes; this account was opened in my husband's name. When SARVAM Coordinators came to give condolences on my husband's death, they asked me about my husband's bank passbook. They explained to me that when they had helped me open the bank account, they had also registered my husband's name in insurance schemes which meant that I would be able to receive 4 lac rupees as a compensation. With this 4 lac rupee I was able to invest 2 lacs each on both of my daughter's names in the bank. I wanted to see my daughters receive education in future and this money helped me safeguard their dreams. I am grateful to SARVAM.

agriculture loan and loans obtained to meet emergency needs—in that order. 60 per cent of the DS families do not approach non-bank sources. The remaining 40 per cent do approach for obtaining loans for meeting the household expenses; educational needs and family functions.

About 50 per cent of the DS interviewed owe a loan ranging from Rs. 25,000-50,000; followed by 34 per cent that owe loan ranging from Rs.10,000-25,000. Everyone owes a minimum of Rs.10,000 loan. About 50 per cent of them have taken loan on mortgage of property. The asset or property mortgaged is gold. There are a few cases where land, and house have also been mortgaged.

Insurance: Almost all the DS have at least three insurance covers, viz. Life insurance, Accident insurance, and Health insurance. It's interesting to note some have insured crop and house also, perhaps it is a new practice coming up recently. The monthly insurance premium paid by 56 per cent of the DS is below Rs. 1,000; whereas there are 43 per cent of them, who pay a premium amount ranging from Rs. 1,000-2,000. All of them avail pension scheme of the government, i.e. NPS.

Use of Smart Phone: Most DS—apart from calling and messaging—use Smartphone for online shopping, online bill payments; and for being on the social media. About 87 per cent of them use it for web browsing; and 70 per cent of them use for internet banking also.

Online Banking: The awareness of DS on online banking facilities is very high. Almost everyone knows about ATMs, branch operations, bank correspondents, pensions, insurance, and net banking, except Credit cards that very few of them use. They use all cashless modes of payments available to them. Reportedly, they use digital transactions more than once a week. They have used all cashless modes of payment, except only 18 per cent of them have used a credit card.

Money transfer and making payments are carried out online by DS, which before becoming a DS, her household members used to do by visiting a bank branch prior to their becoming DS. Their view on the benefits of online transactions is: It's easier, quicker, and convenient to use. Therefore, they always use digital transactions. Everyone of the DS interviewed was found to be familiar with digital transactions, and they do not find any challenges in using such online banking services.

Familiarity with Government Schemes: When listed out various schemes of the government, almost all of them reported that they were aware of all such schemes. Being aware of is one, availing is another. In the case of DS, almost all of them have availed PMJBY, PMSBY, and

APY. However, about 16 per cent; and 22 per cent have not availed Health Insurance, and MGNREGS benefits respectively. There are other schemes such as PMUDY, SGY etc. availed only by about 50 per cent of them or less.

Sustainability: In the event of Digital Sakthi programme stopping, 100 per cent of the DS responded that they would continue to help people with digital transactions; over 90 per cent said that they would either start their own venture or continue to spread the awareness of digital transactions.

They expressed confidence that they would be able to earn something like Rs. 3,000-4,000 per month by involving themselves in such work. They spend nearly four hours daily, offering digital transactions related services and awareness to community members. They expressed also that their household members are supportive to their work.

Income and Savings: About 94 per cent of the DS earn a monthly income of Rs. 4,000-5,000. About 6 per cent of them earn up to Rs. 6,000 a month. Their income levels reportedly have gone up. About 55 per cent of them save Rs.1,000-2,000 monthly, and the remaining 45 per cent save less than Rs. 1,000 a month. The habit of saving is found in everyone of them.

Leadership & Job Preparedness: The leadership training helped improve education, health and self-confidence of DS. Soft skills acquired through SARVAM include Communication Skills, Leadership Skills, Conflict Management Skills, and Achievement Motivation Skills. With regard to the competencies for job preparedness, the DS rate themselves on 4 or 5 in a rating scale ranging from 1-5, where 5 indicates Excellent competency. With regard to computer literacy nearly 72 per cent of them are either 'excellent' or 'very good'; and reportedly others are good. Everyone believes that being computer literate is very important to serve as Digital Sakhi. Almost everyone is also aware of essential computer hardware components of a computer.

Out of 82 DS interviewed, 78 of them use search engines in internet; 74 of them use internet for finding information; and 62 of them use it for purposes, such as WhatsApp, Facebook etc. With regard to various login credentials while signing up the web pages for providing services to beneficiaries, 30 DS who run Digital Seva Kendra expressed that they knew. They have been formally trained in browsing web pages, and signing up, and signing in various portals for offering services using public domains. Others do not know because they are not keeping in touch with computers nor are they accessing various web pages on a day-to-day basis.

All the 30 DS who run Seva Kendra are aware that in order to run/ operate a Seva Kendra a special training and certification are required. They (30 of them who run Seva Kendra) also knew that passing the required courses help to run Digital Seva Kendra.

Everyone of the DS has got awareness on Covid-19 appropriate behaviour. All of them got vaccinated—two doses. The training plus having been vaccinated has increased confidence level to carry out field work in the community. Most of them take up leadership in organising community level development initiatives. They expressed comfortability in having to make a speech or interacting with community members.

Everyone interviewed expressed that they are not taken aback having to make tough decisions, as well as feeling confident in negotiating skills across different socio-political settings. That the community members listen and extend respect to the words of DS stand as testimony for their work make sense to the community.

This extends to operate within the families of DS, that the family members consult them or allow them to make important decisions, including financial decisions pertaining to the family.

Part-2: Women Entrepreneurs

Occupation: Most of the women entrepreneurs reported agriculture, running petty business, cattle rearing and tailoring as their current occupation, which also includes wage employment under the MGNREGS. When asked about the multiple occupations the women entrepreneurs are involved, repeatedly MGNREGS comes as response from many, in addition to being involved in agriculture and petty business they are undertaking.

Income-Expenditure-Savings: With regard to their income, expenditure, and savings, it was found that their expenditures are below their incomes, and their savings range from Rs.1,000-2,000. Everyone interviewed reported that their income increased as a result of Digital Sakhi programme. They save money in multiple ways such as through SHGs, Banks, Post Office, and through local chit funds etc. Some buy gold and assets as well, as a way of saving and investing. However, those who buy gold as a way of saving are very few.

Digital Sakhi: Every entrepreneur interviewed (208 of them) is aware of Digital Sakhi programme. They have attended training programmes organised by the Digital Sakhi Programme. All of them reported that they own a Smartphone. Secondly, in 71 per cent of the families two members owned smartphones; and in 21 per cent of the families at least one smartphone was available. There are 8 per cent of the families where three members owned smartphones.

> **Sangeetha**
>
> I am 28 years old and I have studied till 12th standard. I got married and my husband is working in a private company. I have 2 children who are studying in school. My husband is earning very little and we are leading a normal life. We do not have an android phone in our house and I do not know what all I can do with it. During the Covid-19 lockdown, we purchased an android mobile phone for my children to attend the online classes.
>
> At this time, SARVAM staff came to our house and explained to us about Digital Financial Literacy and asked me what all we can do with the help of android mobile phones. I was amazed after learning what all can be done with the android mobile phones and started using them. I have never used even an ATM card in my life so far but after the training and motivation I have started using ATM and UPI payments such as BHIM, PHONEPE and PAYTM.
>
> I am now helping many people in my village to pay their bills, recharge their mobile phones and various other simple aspects by getting little charges. I am also helping to order many things online and this has given me more confidence and my respect has increased a lot amongst the village people. Thanks a lot to SARVAM.

Smartphone Use: 100 per cent of them know how to use a Smartphone. All of them have got their mobile numbers linked to their bank accounts. Over 90 per cent of them use Smartphone for making calls, messaging, paying bills, for online shopping, and for accessing social media. Those who use it for net banking or browsing are less than 50 per cent.

Borrowings: Main source of borrowing are SHGs, Banks, MFIs, and LTFS. No one seems to approach local moneylenders or pawn brokers for borrowing, which is a good thing to note.

Loan to Repay: Out of 208 entrepreneurs interviewed, 198 have borrowed through some source or the other. All of them, reportedly, have borrowed for the purpose of small business. They also expressed that they have difficulty in repaying. Only 10 of them have not borrowed.

Insurance: Everyone (208) has Accident Insurance; 92-93 per cent of them have either Health insurance or Life Insurance. There are some (10%) who have insured their livestock, and others (6%) have insured crop. More than 97 per cent of them avail NPS run by government; and six per cent of them invest in pension scheme offered by private MFIs, and banks.

Entrepreneurial Activities: The type of business activities that the entrepreneurs are engaged in are: running petty shops, tailoring, sale of agri products, sale of milk. All of them feel comfortable in running

Akhila

I am 21 years old and I have completed only 5th standard. I am a physically handicapped woman who is not allowed outside to do any work because of my physical inability. I used to sit idle inside my house without doing anything. One day I got an opportunity to attend a skill training conducted by SARVAM on tailoring which helped me to learn more aspects related to modern tailoring. This gave me confidence and the Tamil Nadu Government gave me a tailoring machine under the help for physically handicapped persons. I am using the machine and with the skills I have learnt through the skill training programme, I have started to gain income now.

I am happy that I am able to stitch more dresses and many customers are giving their dresses for stitching. I am thankful to SARVAM for changing my life in a positive manner.

their business. Regarding growth and development of business, everyone's response is: '*incremental growth/small progression*'. What it implies is that there is neither decline nor great acceleration.

A simple 'Before-After' comparison of number of customers, who visit the entrepreneurs for purchase or for availing services show a shift from 10-20 to 20-30 or 30-40. There is a progression noticed in the number of customers they have been able to attract.

The change in annual income shows that after joining the Digital Sakthi Programme, the income levels have gone up from Rs. 10,000-20,000 bracket to Rs. 20,000-30,000 bracket. For about 7 per cent of them, it has touched Rs. 30,000-40,000 bracket. Thus, in the income brackets, there is a positive change the data reveal.

With regard to saving, 64 per cent of the entrepreneurs save Rs. 1,000-2,000 per month; 26 per cent of them save Rs. 2,000-3,000; and about 10 per cent of them save more than Rs. 3,000 a month.

About 50 per cent of the entrepreneurs get external orders also for delivery. They include orders some of them (20%) get from super markets for agri products; and tailoring orders women tailors get (25%) from schools and big shops etc. There are other types of business that depends on local demand and local customers.

Digital Banking: Everyone of the entrepreneur is aware of all the banking facilities, except that a few of them (3%) are unaware of net banking facility. Everyone of entrepreneur is aware of (and use) cashless modes of payments, except that some (5%) are not aware of credit card use. Ninety one per cent use digital cashless transactions on a weekly basis; and 8 per cent use at least once in a fortnight.

Almost in every entrepreneur's family members of the family are availing banking services, except that they are not availing net banking services. Among the cashless modes of payment, Debit cards, AEPS, and UPI are frequently used by many entrepreneurs followed by USSD or mobile wallets like PayTM/PhonePe. With regard to the benefits of digital transactions, everyone responded: Easy to use, Quicker, Convenient, and Time saving. There's none who doesn't know the benefits. No one among the entrepreneurs find digital transactions challenging.

COVID-19: Amidst widely spreading myths and misinformation about COVID-19, this survey found that the entrepreneurs have correct and fact-based information about COVID-19. However, regarding vaccination, it was found that nine of them have got only one dose of vaccine at the time of this survey.

The knowledge of COVID-19 appropriate behaviour among the entrepreneurs was found to be correct and fact-based, as reported by almost all of them. They have primarily got these information, awareness and motivation to go for vaccination through Digital Sakhis. This programme was running amidst COVID-19 pandemic. Thus, there is reference to COVID-19, and community members response to the pandemic.

Part-3: Community Members

Occupation & Income: The current occupation, as reported by most of the community members is *daily wage employment.* There are others, comparatively small in number involved in tailoring and farming, and running their own grocery or vegetable stalls. The primary sources of income to most members of the community are: daily wage labourers, being employed in private jobs, farming, or tailoring—in that order.

For 45 per cent of the community members, their total monthly income is in the range of Rs. 5,000-7,000; for 40 per cent it's in the range of Rs. 7,000-9,000. There are very few who earn more than Rs. 9,000 per month. Forty six per cent of them save anywhere between Rs. 1,001-2,000; while 10 per cent of them save Rs. 500 or less.

Digital Sakhi Programme: All the 326 community members interviewed, reported to have known about Digital Sakhi Programme.

Vasanthy Jagadeeswaran, Kadaperikuppam, 42 years' old

In our lives, education plays a pivotal role in shaping the perspective of others in society. This was the understanding based on my experience living as a high school graduate married into a family of college graduates. The self-worth that comes with accessing higher education and the opportunity it provides was missing in my life. My husband worked in private sector while my in-laws were government employees. As someone who couldn't complete her secondary school education, I hesitated to voice my opinion, even if I were given a chance to. I felt as an outsider in my own family, inferior to everyone else with their college diplomas and degrees. This was my life before I found myself attending a training and motivation programme organized by SARVAM. This one step changed how I viewed myself and instead of feeling like a victim of circumstances, I decided to take charge of my life. Becoming a volunteer in SARVAM was my calling, my high school diploma was a good enough qualification for me to become part of training and other motivation programmes. My family members were astonished by the people especially women praising and thanking me and my ability planning and started to giving respect to me as well. I felt valued and thanks to SARVAM. In my family, community and society in general honoring me. I am a volunteer now, who wakes up everyday to meet and teach villagers guiding them to live a life defined not by lack of opportunities, but by their aspirations.

All of them have attended training programmes conducted under Digital Sakhi banner.

Everyone of them reported that their savings has increased after their association with Digital Sakhi Programme. Community members have more than one option to keep their savings. Majority use (i) bank accounts, (ii) SHG account, (iii) or Post Office. There are some who save through private chit funds.

Smartphone: Ninety one per cent of the entrepreneurs reported to own a smartphone, while others reported that they do not have one, although their family members have and use one. However, 99 per cent of them reported to know about how to use a smartphone. Everyone who owns a mobile phone has linked their phone number to their bank accounts.

Interestingly, in 79 per cent of the households there are two or three smartphones; in 20 per cent of the houses there is at least one phone available. There is hardly one per cent that does not have a smartphone. Possibly, they have ordinary handsets. The community members use smartphones for purposes such as calling, paying bills online, messaging, accessing social media, and for online shopping. The least used online services are web browsing or net banking.

Borrowing: Eighty five per cent of the respondents had borrowed from various sources at the time when this survey was conducted. Hardly 15 per cent reported not owing any money to anyone at all. On the source of borrowing by the community members, SHGs come on the priority. There are other Institutional sources such as banks, MFIs, cooperatives, LTFS in the next line of order. It's good to note that their dependence on pawn brokers and moneylenders is the least.

Insurance: With regard to insurance, most of them had insured against accident, some had life insurance, vehicle insurance, and health insurance. It was reported by some that they had insured crops and livestock also. Understandably, some had multiple insurance. All the community members interviewed availed the pension scheme run by the government, i.e. NPS. There is hardly anyone who had availed private pension schemes run by banks or MFI.

Budgeting: All the community members in this sample reported that they have the practice of making monthly budgeting, although often not written up. Everyone thinks it is useful and wise idea to do a financial planning to be able to keep expenses under control, and for considering savings plans. All the respondents of this survey reported that they were involved in financial decisions of their family.

Banking Services: With regard to their awareness of banking/financial facilities, it was found that almost everyone interviewed reported to be aware of ATMs, pension scheme, insurance scheme, banking correspondents—including net banking. Awareness level with regard to the cashless modes of payment is very high. Reportedly, everyone knows about Debit cards, AEPS, UPI, Mobile wallets such as PayTM, USSD and credit cards.

Digital Transactions: Almost everyone interviewed reported to be using digital cashless transactions. However, the frequency of use differed. Most of them (78%) use weekly; some (20%) use fortnightly; and a few (2%) use monthly etc. It was found cashless transactions are progressively and rapidly becoming part of their day-to-day financial practice.

Everyone or almost everyone interviewed reported to be availing all banking/financial services. The most frequently used cashless mode of payments are: debit cards, AEPS, and UPI followed by USSD and mobile wallets. The number of people who use credit cards are very few. Benefits perceived in digital transactions are: easier, quicker, convenient, and time saving.

Ninety seven per cent do not feel any challenge in using digital banking, whereas a few expressed challenges of connectivity. There is a negligible few that expressed cyber-crime stories they heard about, which wean them off from trying digital transactions.

Gowri, Perambai, 50 years

In my early 20s, I got married but soon after my husband left me alone with our only son. He never returned home but he left me with a trauma of being an abandoned woman. Living in a village where even widows have more respect than a woman left by her husband, I suffered mental agony for years that followed. I had resigned to my fate and this way of life till one day a motivation programme was conducted in our village by SARVAM. Attending that programme opened my eyes. As if waking from a slumber, I saw the world around me had changed over all these years. This encouraged me to attend the training and become a tailor and started work in my house itself. I, who would be anxious about visiting markets alone, now go out to teach and educate several people on importance of confidence. My villagers and family members respect me now and see me as a success, more importantly I don't feel abandoned. Although as a single mother I have been living an independent life all these years, thanks to SARVAM, I have embraced that spirit of freedom within for the very first time and can call it a successful life.

Government Schemes: Although most of the respondents know about the social security schemes, majority of them have availed only a few of the schemes such as PMSBY, PMJJBY, APY, PM-JAY and MGNREGS. Other schemes such as PMUY, PM-Kisan, PMMY-Mudra have been availed by very few.

Digital Sakhi: People consult and take the services of Digital Sakhis, as reported by everyone. In most cases, the average time spent by Digital Sakhis in each visit is 1-2 hours.

COVID-19: Most of the community members have got COVID-19 appropriate behaviour related awareness and vaccination assistance only through Digital Sakhis. The training programmes of SARVAM, TV and social media, besides friends and family members have been the main sources of COVID-19 related awareness—apart from the awareness and assistance provided by the Digital Sakhis.

Everyone reported that they got vaccination awareness mainly through Digital Sakhis. This has motivated 92 per cent of the community members to have got 2 jabs of COVID-19 prevention vaccine, and the others have got at least one jab. There is none who still remained unvaccinated.

Confidence Level and Community Leadership: Eighty one per cent expressed that their confidence level increased because of their association with Digital Sakhi programme. About 19 per cent felt that sometimes they feel confident, and at other times, they tend to think that they need to develop further confidence.

Sixty four per cent of the community members 'always' feel that they are ready to take up leadership roles in communities. Thirty six per cent feel they sometimes feel so, and at other times, feel that they are not ready yet. They might need further training and exposure. Sixty per cent 'always' feel comfortable when they have to make a presentation to a crowd. Others (40%) sometimes feel comfortable, and other times not so. Sixty nine per cent 'always' feel comfortable even in taking *tough decisions*, while 31 per cent 'sometimes' feel comfortable and at other times tough being uncomfortable. Seventy four per cent 'always' feel that others respect them in the community; while 26 per cent 'sometimes' feel others respecting them. Seventy four per cent reported involving themselves in the financial decisions of their families; while 26 per cent reported that 'sometimes' they are involved and not always.

Assistance to the Ultra-poor

SARVAM, employing participatory methods, identifies the marginalized households (in other words the poorest of the poor in the villages) and helps them in many ways. They include providing educational loan assistance to children of such families so that they will not have to discontinue their studies no matter how

adverse the conditions at home. Girls studying in nearby village high schools are given bicycles on loan to commute to school daily. Such families are also encouraged and trained to take up additional income earning activities such as goat-rearing,

incense stick manufacturing, pickle making and packing, coconut leaf thatch plaiting, bicycle repairing, tailoring, running a laundry, public telephone booth, or other small businesses. Besides these, widows who were confined to their kitchens have come out to participate in SARVAM activities and have come to realize that they have been given a new lease of life in coming together and participating.

MARGINALIZED SECTIONS OF SOCIETY

Families of barbers and washermen belong to sections of the marginalized community in Tamil Nadu. They render a service that the villagers want. But as the years go by the number of families that offer such services in villages have come down drastically. Those who continue to do these occupations require improving the way they work, and they need newer tools to work with. SARVAM's Community Revolving Fund has helped barbers buy new tools to work with; and the washermen have replaced their old-iron box with newer ones and also pushcarts, which can be used as ironing tables as well as pushcarts, making it easier to move around in the villages and render their services. The participation of women from such marginalized communities has enabled them to obtain loans for such purposes, which they repay promptly.

Interface with Local Bodies

Manaveli Model Village: One of the hamlets, Manaveli, was promoted to serve as a model for other hamlets to emulate. SARVAM, through systematic intervention, has brought about several changes both in terms of facilities and outlook of community members. Their intervention ranged from revitalising the local preschool to improvement of school infrastructure, and common facilities such as the community hall, and water supply; as well as family level facilities like housing and sanitation. Specific interventions for the development of youth and women and

INTERFACE WITH ELECTED BODIES

Under the Panchayati Raj System government departments work through elected Village Panchayats (VP) with the Village Panchayat Presidents dealing with each department of the government on behalf of the community. Since the VP President gradually becomes the sole point of contact for all the departments, it happens sometimes, that VP Presidents develop a tendency to make decisions on behalf of the community —for example preparation of the list of beneficiaries for a given programme. They convince the other Panchayat functionaries to adhere to her/his decisions. Since SARVAM goes by the criteria fixed by local committees (in which of course, the Panchayat President is also a member), it sometimes does not go in line with the way the Panchayat President wants it. It has caused Panchayat Presidents to become apprehensive; and disapprove of the list (of participants) recommended by the local committee as prospective participants for a given programme. This is something that the SARVAM team has to constantly face and resolve. At times, it has resulted in an elected Panchayat President not cooperating with or being unresponsive to the developmental initiatives of the SARVAM Team.

The approach of the SARVAM team has been that SARVAM will respect the elected local body, and be unconcerned about anyone person being unhappy or indifferent. It will go along with the decision of the local committee in which the Panchayat President and other local leaders are members. This fair-mindedness and abstaining from direct involvement and allowing the local committees to make decisions have also served as plus-points for SARVAM to move ahead successfully in the fieldwork.

for children such as the children's corner have been initiated. Women have been motivated to participate in diversified livelihood activities. Saving habits and proper use of revolving funds have also been instituted. Programmes such as periodical health camps and annual summer camps for school children have also been arranged. Enhanced milk production and kitchen gardens have contributed to variety in the nutritional intake of the people. Manaveli has indeed become a model village for other hamlets to emulate.

Local Decision-making: SARVAM—taking into consideration the limited financial resources it was able to mobilize for its village development programmes—had paid utmost attention to the poorest, and given priority to the marginalized families in the community. The criteria fixed for selection of participants for each programme—be it housing or provision of dairy cow—was fairly and squarely laid on locally formed committees. They included a Housing Committee, Livelihoods Committee, Committee for Sanction of Community Funds and so on. Problems had cropped up for in any rural community everyone thinks her/his family is poor too. Everyone tends to ask: 'Am I not poor too?' However, the local committee managed to handle them, instead of SARVAM pitching in. This has further reinforced SARVAM's interest in the poorest families, and its genuine respect for local decisions.

Media for Social Change

A monthly village journal, *Grama Pudiya Udayam*, was launched in February 2007 to publish stories from services villages. It goes on successfully even now in 2023. It carries positive messages, messages of the Mother, and progress being made by families and children in the service villages. The news organization and management was originally done by the village youth with support from SARVAM. Perhaps, because it is their news, the response for the journal from the community is overwhelming.

People's participation in contributing news items to the magazine, and motivating the youth not only to write but also to emulate positive and constructive activities being taken up in other hamlets, villages and districts is admirable. This journal also provides space for SARVAM to spread word about its programmes and seek the opinion of the community members on new activities planned.

People feel happy to read about their village development stories through this journal in their vernacular. Out of the 1000 copies printed

COMMUNITY JOURNAL

SARVAM has introduced a monthly community journal in Tamil, the *Grama Pudhiya Udhayam*, meaning [Rural/Village] *New Dawn*. 1000 copies are printed every month. This is an innovative venture that serves several purposes. It helps put across development news from all the villages where SARVAM works. Many local youths write in that journal. It gives them immense pleasure to see their thoughts in print, and since it is read by many, it helps to share ideas so community members will read and realise how others in their locality use the services of SARVAM or the government of Tamil Nadu to get out of poverty; how families and communities use developmental assistance; and how people diversify their livelihoods in order to get out of poverty. It also publishes names of participants selected for various programmes, which is a means to ensure transparency and prove that SARVAM is being accountable. This journal serves also to train local youth in responsible reportage.

about 700 are circulated within the village and the rest go to the government offices in the district. It is priced at Rs. 1 per issue. There are also local people who have taken annual subscription to this journal.

Community Centre

In 2007, SARVAM built a multi-purpose community centre, Satyam, in Poothurai village. The various functions that this centre fulfils are as follows:

- A meeting and activity centre for all kinds of groups: women, children, youth, farmers, community workers etc.;
- A library, reading room and television room;
- An auditorium where cultural and fine arts programmes, educational films and multimedia shows are held;
- A village information centre with Internet access to provide information useful to the villagers; and
- A silent contemplation room, a space for spiritual communion.

Network and Collaboration

The social, capital and official connections that Poothurai and Perambai have established while the Village Development Project was being implemented by SARVAM is commendable. Those village leaders who took active part in the activities of SARVAM must have discovered social and official connections can take their villages to great heights, provided they use these connections honestly for social development causes. They are in touch with many departments of the government; many government officials know that these two villages are model villages established with the assistance of SARVAM; the community members are in touch with several hospitals and these hospitals hold periodical health camps in these villages; the community members have been introduced to insurance companies of repute and many of them have life and health insurance cover. If the community leaders are smart enough, they should be able to make these benefits last long even after SARVAM phases itself out.

Sharanam: Centre for Sustainable Rural Transformation

Sharanam, the Centre for Sustainable Rural Transformation, is essentially a training centre constructed with a vision of sharing with larger groups of communities in Tamil Nadu, other parts of India and beyond, the experiences of SARVAM and learning from them. It will take up regular training programmes, extension activities, and research programmes, especially those that help build necessary skills among rural community leaders. Thus, an innovative programme of rural 'transformative leaders' is being designed. The centre has become operational from March 2014. This facility is being used by other national institutions such as National Institute of Rural Development & Panchayati Raj (NIRDPR), as a peaceful ambience to conduct training, seminars and conferences. We discuss about Sharanam in another section below.

Additional Hands that Extend Help

Village Development Programme of SARVAM drew visitors from many fields of development and some of them, including the Government of Tamil Nadu, chipped in with their contributions for the cause of rural transformation within the broad ideals of Sri Aurobindo Society. Some of them are given below.

Project Ringtone: This is a unique initiative started in partnership with Hewlett-Packard (HP). It is basically a computer awareness programme for school children. Started with the aim of creating expertise

among the village students to design mind-maps of stories and turn them into computer animations, the programme is going very successfully. Training is given to children in the age group of 10-16 years, primarily in two open source applications—'Movie Soup' and 'Scratch'.

US Embassy Micro Scholarship Programme: Under the aegis of the US Embassy, the Village Development Project has started a new English Micro Scholarship Programme that provides a foundation of English language skills to economically disadvantaged 13-20 years old through 2 years of instructions and intensive sessions. This programme goes on for quite some years now very successfully. So far, over 450 rural children got benefit from this programme.

Health and Sanitation: The Village Development Programme has established connections with premier hospitals—JIPMER, PIMS, SLIMS, Aravind Eye Hospital—in Pondicherry and Tamil Nadu. They conduct periodical health camps and free surgeries for patients from Poothurai and Perambai. The Swachh Bharat Mission Programme of the Government of Tamil Nadu also has extended a helping hand for 100 sanitation works in the project area.

The Loomba Foundation: The Loomba Foundation provides additional support to the women empowerment works of SARVAM, known as 'Socio-economic Empowerment of Widows Project'. It has helped to promote the mission of empowering women, especially widows, economically and also to bring them into the mainstream of national life.

Power of Collective Aspiration: JIPMER, India's premier medical education and research institute, is 13 km by road from Poothurai village. There existed from Poothurai, an age-old cart-track through which JIPMER was only 2.8 km away. This passed through community-owned land but it could not be used due to long-standing encroachments of various kinds.

Unfortunately, nobody had the vision, or will to take advantage of this track for linking up with JIPMER for by having access to JIPMER in 30 minutes by walking or 15 minutes by cycling the village would get a quantum jump to a world-class super speciality medical care, where service is free of cost. It was a time when Poothurai village did not have access even to primary health care. The idea of the road's potential was eventually planted into the collective consciousness of the community, resulting in a genuine aspiration for implementation of the idea.

A proposal was presented to the District Collector who happened to visit the village. Since the entire issue was laid within his direct jurisdiction, he immediately set the proposal in motion, spurred his subordinates to act swiftly and subsequently sanctioned the work on the link road with an outlay of Rs.50 lakh. The cart-track has now become a tar-road and JIPMER is just 2.8 kms away.

SARVAM's Strategic Plan 2014–2020 showed the way forward to expand SARVAM's activities to other neighbourhood villages also. It was a participatory visionary exercise to implement the mechanisms that can replicate and scale up SARVAM's work to the neighbourhood villages and blocks. SARVAM works in about sixty villages as of 2023. With the financial and technical support of institutions such as L&TFS, TCS, HDFC, and US Embassy is making it possible.

Strategies that Work

India, particularly Tamil Nadu State has been putting to use several approaches and strategies for rural development. They include a wide array, each of which pins down faith in different institutions—some in social institutions such as community-based organizations; some on local institutions of governance such as Panchayats; yet others on economic institutions such as banks and cooperatives, a fourth on bureaucratic institutions such as Block Development Offices; others on development agencies such as NGOs, and more recently, also for profit development institutions.

In terms of approach, both the government and the NGOs have attempted several approaches. They include integrated approaches, sector-specific approaches, target-group approaches, area-approaches and so on. SARVAM has put in efforts to implement a concept called Integral Development Approach.

Now, to return to our question of how development takes place. Does it take place as part of social dynamics and politico-economic transactions? Or is it the way development practitioners facilitate development and strategize community action? Is it about fulfilling the felt-needs of the community at a time when its absence was severely felt? You can call it development; you can call it transformation. What is important is what has happened to 'the way people think and transact and interact', and 'what it has resulted in'. What strategies and development methods helped SARVAM achieve what they have got going on the ground today in Poothurai and Perambai? One important differentiator was that there was no rush or desperation in our search for achievements. It was small, deliberate steps with a clear vision and meditative focus.

An institution or an individual can influence development to some extents, based on a certain concept/ideology or scheme of things. There is always a relationship between the thought one implants and the transformation one looks forward to witness in a given community.

We shall see in the following chapters the kind of transformation SARVAM has caused to take place in the service villages. There is an epilogue section that exclusively captures the transformation process. Let us move on to the next chapter and get to know what SARVAM has come out with and the distinctive lessons it has to offer on development practice.

Chapter 4

The Tenets of Transformation

SARVAM believes that the shaping of consciousness is the fundamental source of social change, which results in rural transformation. The activities of SARVAM, and the constant interaction of SARVAM field staff with the community members, especially with women and children have brought about considerable change in the way people think, live and transact. In this chapter, we make an attempt to deduce some key lessons from SARVAM's Village Development Project.

Development in Practice

How did SARVAM choose to start work in Poothurai and Perambai? The usual approach to commence development work is to look for a village where people are generally reported to be 'cooperative' and where problems reported are simple and not too complex to comprehend or address. But SARVAM's assertion has been different. SARVAM had come to know that Poothurai and Perambai Panchayats were difficult to deal with because of the non-cooperative nature of the local people, and problems were so many that it might be difficult to comprehend and chalk out a development direction, whether participatory or top-down. Those who knew about these villages had cautioned SARVAM not to get involved with the problems. If involved, SARVAM would be dragged deeply into the sludge of problems. The people described the two villages as "drunkards' villages", if we can quote verbatim. They cautioned the SARVAM team that the results were going to be discouragingly slow in coming.

Despite all the cautions given the SARVAM team decided to take up Poothurai and Perambai for three distinct reasons: (i) one gets the satisfaction of having done something meaningful only if one can make a difference in a place where people are neck deep in problems;

(ii) ***the aspiration to get on the development path exists in every individual and thus in every community. All that is needed is for the community in question to clearly find a genuine commitment in the hands that are extending the help; and*** (iii) a resolute faith in the divine. The sequencing of activities that SARVAM planned and carried out could be a contribution to development of these two villages, and those in the neighbourhood.

Sequence of the Entry Point Activities: The entry point activities and sequencing of activities that SARVAM used in order to get down to working with the community are good lessons in development practices. SARVAM began working with children in the first place, starting with school children, pre-school children, and high school children. In order to orient mothers on 'child development' SARVAM convened meetings of mothers, where they educated the women on child health, nutrition, child care and so on. When the activities with children drew the attention of the women, they too started participating and sharing their concerns on issues that went beyond child rearing and child development.

Secondly, SARVAM moved on to discuss poverty and other livelihood concerns of women and families, which had surfaced constantly during the women's meetings. This resulted in the commencement of livelihood support activities and initiation of the community revolving fund.

Thirdly, it moved on to work with the youth, involving them in social development activities as volunteers. The youth thus found their association with SARVAM and which gave them a special status in the village, and a change in the way they think and act. They found themselves being useful not only to the community but also to their families in due course. Gradually, everyone in the community started participating in the Health Camps, veterinary camps and livelihood activities. SARVAM found that, after working with them for a while, everyone in these seven hamlets wanted to get out of the poverty muddle they were in.

Cadbury lends a helping hand: SARVAM started its work in a small way in February 2005, with just one person, very little financial and infrastructural resources, but with big dreams and high aspirations. ***From the beginning, a decision was taken that their entry into the village would be relaxed and SARVAM would keep a low profile. The stress was on interacting with the villagers so as to win their confidence and trust at every level.*** It was in 2006 that Cadbury Schweppes started partnering SARVAM in their village development initiatives. Before

Cadburys' support, the choice of activities was based on the urgency of a particular need in a given situation and was influenced by the availability of financial resources.

CADBURY EMPLOYEES PARTICIPATE

Cadbury has gone beyond financial support, offering moral support and developmental guidance. Mr. Venkatesan Chandramouli, Director, India Snacking Ltd. has always been encouraging and advising the Village Development Project staff. He always mentions that SARVAM is a flagship programme for Mondelez International. In 2007, Mr. Anand Kripalu, Managing Director, Cadbury India Ltd. visited the Village Development Project. The same year a team of 35 sales executives from Cadbury India Ltd. led by Mr. Ransom D'Souza visited the project. They observed the integral development taking place, learnt a great deal, shared views and suggestions for improving the nutritional intake of the villagers and how to improve the quality of education in rural schools. Ms. Susan Georgie, Manager CSR from Cadbury visited the Village Development Project in September 2013. She showed interest in bringing Cadbury employees as volunteers to participate in and contribute towards a series of week-long children's programmes to be conducted by the Village Development Project.

SARVAM's work took a quantum leap and gathered an increasing momentum with the coming of Cadbury Schweppes as partners and collaborators. The approach of Cadbury Schweppes was entirely different from the usual approach of sponsors but it was in tune with the ideals of SARVAM, which was based on a genuine commitment to do something lasting and worthwhile for the village community. The scope of SARVAM's interventions expanded.

Social Infrastructure: Infrastructure refers to the basic facilities, services and installations needed for the functioning of a community or society. One smart development strategy is focusing on social infrastructure as a key success factor in enhancing community well-being. To put it a little more elaborately, we can say social infrastructure refers to community facilities, services and networks that help individuals, families, groups and communities meet their social needs, maximize their potential for development, and enhance community well-being. They include universal facilities and services such as education, training, health, welfare, social services, open space, recreation and sports, learning, arts and cultural facilities; civic and democratic institutions; and community meeting places.

Ensuring availability of essential social infrastructure and access to service provision has enabled communities in the SARVAM villages to have sufficient resources to develop and enhance their economic, social, cultural and environmental well-being. A range of providers of social infrastructure, including related government departments, have been generous in their assistance to the service villages of SARVAM.

Building Social Infrastructure: SARVAM got down to the building and renovation of social infrastructure such as school buildings, *anganwadi* centres, building of community hall, construction of roads (with assistance of the government, of course); and then moved on to help individual families construct toilets, renovate houses etc. Subsequently, SARVAM initiated livelihood diversification and promotion/other economic programmes. This is the uniqueness of working with untied funds. The funds allotted from the government are usually tied to a specific purpose, to be spent before a specified timeline. It undermines the idea of participatory planning. Instead it brings in an urgency to disburse the funds and report in the relevant web portal—fund utilized. The fund made available by Cadbury to SARVAM had no conditions and was meant for any rural development purpose. Therefore, SARVAM was able to make use of the funds giving priority to the felt-needs of the people, on a demand-driven basis. Also community financial participation was an imperative in all the programmes of SARVAM.

Social infrastructure provides the means to measure the status of a people or community, including:

- Sense of identity—from housing, community hall, reading rooms, engaged in a chosen livelihood activity, and other arts and sports activities;

- Sense of belonging and inclusion—achieved from both the presence of the facilities and the activities that occur within them, e.g. being a member of a local committee, being considered for a project or programme by the local committee, taking part in common space activities and sports;

- An educated community—preschools, primary, intermediate and secondary education, and tertiary education;
- Networking and community interaction—in events, local networks and activities;
- Democratic participation and citizenship—voting, standing for election, seeking consensus, taking part in civic affairs, free deliberation about common developmental problems;
- Physical and mental health—from health service provision to the facilities that encourage physical activity and/or social interaction, e.g. community festivals, sports and plays, summer camp activities, and use of community centres;

- Spiritual and cultural well-being—learning to respect one another, cooperate, learn tolerance, learn to listen, inner-search, respecting women, cultural and spiritual organisations, networks and facilities etc.; and
- Creative expression—through art and painting, computer animation, dance forms, writing for community journal etc.

Investment in social infrastructure is essential for the health, well-being and economic prosperity of communities. It plays an important role in bringing people together, maintaining quality of life and developing the skills and resilience essential to strong communities.

- Enhance lifestyles of communities;
- Provide for the social needs of the people;
- Provide efficient and affordable infrastructure; and
- Helps implement an efficient and integrated planning for village development.

Scale of Intervention: Initially, the scale of SARVAM's intervention was small, covering only seven hamlets. This could be attributed as a factor contributing to the success of SARVAM. When the scale is small; it is easier to bring about change with community participation. SARVAM since the beginning has established its name in these villages as an institution giving top priority to the marginalised sections of society

> **AWARENESS OF GOVERNMENT SCHEMES**
>
> SARVAM, besides implementing programmes commonly in demand from the community, also sources for or helps government officials implement relevant programmes to the right beneficiaries. The relationship SARVAM maintains with various government offices is very useful. There are benefits such as (i) no corruption entailed when SARVAM is involved; (ii) deserving beneficiaries get selected; and (iii) the villagers themselves confidently deal with the scheme implementing officers.

such as those from the Scheduled Caste (SC), and the ultra-poor. The decisions are very much local and rapid.

The Prime Movers

(i) *Excellence in academic performance*: The activities undertaken through supplementary coaching for school children, and additional support rendered to local schools have made local school children show excellent results in school examinations;

(ii) *Excellence in extra-curricular activities*: The activities carried out for school children through summer camps and children's corner have helped children manifest their hidden talents in a vast array of activities such as folk dance, classical dance, art and painting, sports and games, and so on, talents that parents never thought existed in their children; and

(iii) *Self-discipline of children*: Parents have witnessed the self-discipline and positive changes in the way children behave at home and in education-related matters.

These things have served as prime movers in the village. It has helped bring about a positive image of SARVAM in the villages. The parents of these children have started participating in SARVAM's activities in large numbers. Some who were initially unconcerned have started becoming supportive. School drop-out rates have come down. Teachers in Poothurai and Perambai schools started feeling proud of their children's performance. ***Parents who used to send their children to private schools started asking for admission to these government schools, which became an unbelievable development trend in Tamil Nadu.*** Children have been in the forefront in demonstrating that development is possible. The bringing out of their children's multiple talents and academic performance has had a profound influence on parents' cooperation. Children and women thus served as brand ambassadors of SARVAM.

Touching the Bottom of the Society: SARVAM has always worked towards uplifting those living on the edge of poverty, and those marginalised in the society. The decisions, however, have most often been by the local committees, rather than by SARVAM. This is a kind of process-oriented ownership building rather than showing mere development outputs which often become unsustainable.

Decisions by local people or beneficiary selection by local people have reinforced the confidence of the people, and also for the government machinery to come forward and sanction government schemes meant for the poor—be it laying of roads, or construction of household toilets, or housing for the poor. When the beneficiary selection is unbiased, transactions with the government machinery have also been clean and corruption-free—no palm greasing of any government staff. It has facilitated the poor to search internally, and make honest attempts to hold an unbiased view of government officials.

Teaching Healthy Habits: Children learn proper sanitation and personal hygiene habits during the supplementary tuition classes. SARVAM's staff have members demonstrated them the personal hygiene habits such as toilets cleanliness, periodical nail clipping, and washing hands with soap before and after eating. The construction of household toilets and the learnings on the use and maintenance of toilets has helped the women stop the habit of defecating in open places. Although their physical coverage is not full, SARVAM has been able to cultivate clean habits and sanitation culture in the two villages.

Instilling a Sense of Pride: The housing scheme for the poor has been a big success. ***Beneficiary identification was done meticulously to support the marginalised and the ultra-poor who, without SARVAM's support, could never dream of owning a house in their lifetime.*** With funds mobilized and using IAY/PMAY-G, SARVAM has helped 110 families to renovate their houses and about 70 poor families to construct new houses. The ownership of a livable house has given the community a sense of pride, belonging and dignity.

Three significant lessons learnt in the process of carrying out the housing project as an integral part of the village programme were:

First, government machinery is not corrupt as such, provided you are able to develop a trust and prove the point, through your dealings and behaviour, that you are an honest NGO or person working for real village transformation to take place. ***Your being clean benefits the community you serve. Misgivings and distrust tends to create a spiraling effect pushing development efforts down the tunnel making you to entertain crooked thoughts and eventually end up being corrupt.*** If you want others to be honest start being honest yourself. Goodness breeds goodness. Perhaps, this is the reasons the Mother addresses 'Goodness' as a divine quality, one must 'adore'.

Secondly, people, however poor, are willing to work hard and contribute in all possible ways—including financially—if the problem you have taken up is really their felt-need. ***This was seen when the poor community members brought in their hard earned money to contribute financially to get their houses renovated or newly constructed. Therefore, identify what they think they need, and not what you think they need.***

Thirdly, poverty is not all about money and income. The pride of living in one's own house, renovated or newly constructed—no matter how small it is—gets people out of the feeling of being mired in poverty. In fact, they may have taken a loan from SHG for the construction or renovation of the house they live in. They may be indebted and are repaying their debts. They may be financially worse off than they were before. But, the pride of living in one's own house wipes the 'poverty thinking' out of them. They have the urge to repay the loan obtained so as to feel the ownership in full. This is perhaps, what Sri Aurobindo meant when he wanted to have change in 'thinking and being'.

Poothurai and Perambai were villages on the delinquents list of banks that denied loans to anyone who introduced himself/herself as coming from these two villages. That was the impression banks had because of the bitter experiences they underwent during their loan recovery drive. Later, the SARVAM team taught the locals how reliability with banks can take them to great heights. The villagers learnt repayment ethics and proved to the banks through their honest transactions that they are trustworthy, if not credit-worthy. Now they have good rapport with all the banks in the vicinity. **This has brought in a kind of self-awareness, with it the qualities of trust and obedience. Thus, it's only by a change of consciousness that the true basis of life can be discovered**. This is being installed as a *sadhana* in day-to-day life of people engaged by SARVAM—that the whole life is a *sadhana*—be it eating or sleeping.

Linking Institutions with the Community: SARVAM has helped the villagers connect with many public institutions that could be of benefit to them. Thus many popular hospitals, government offices, and local NGOs have been involved in the process of this development. When it

came to the question of laying roads or construction of household toilets, renovation of ponds and tanks, SARVAM has made use of government schemes to carry out such works. For medical assistance SARVAM has brought in the involvement of institutions like JIPMER and Aravind Eye Hospital and they are now working for the people in these villages even in the absence of SARVAM. Similarly, banks and milk producers cooperatives like PONLAIT are very much in the picture. Need-based collaboration with various institutions is something very important for development to take place, and linkage with such institutions has been crucial for sustaining development.

Demand-driven: Most of the programmes implemented are demand-driven. People have made livelihood choices, for which SARVAM has lent a helping hand, offering financial assistance, institutional link-up, marketing collaboration etc. Housing for the poor was another demand, for people were living in houses that were really dilapidated. Therefore, SARVAM partly with the aid of Cadbury's funds and partly through government schemes has introduced housing and household toilet schemes. ***Now it is found that these housing projects have given the people not only a house to live in, but also a sense of dignity, self-respect and responsibility to maintain it properly.*** People wanted the local school to be elevated to a high school, for which SARVAM had taken the necessary steps and made it possible. The projects have thus been always

demand-driven rather than SARVAM planning and offering. SARVAM has facilitated and people have participated and carried out.

Local Decision Making: SARVAM has very deliberately insisted on community decision making in all matters related to local development. ***This has shifted responsibility squarely on to the community to be fully involved and make it a success without any local disputes. One important reason for the success of the housing programme has been the local decision making on beneficiary selection. This has helped develop a participatory culture and democracy in practice at the grassroots level. People learn the social life of democracy.***

Children as Future Assets: SARVAM has considered children as the real future asset of any family/community. Therefore, they have been introduced to a wide range of skills and opportunities to improve their capabilities and academic acumen. The general impression is that the role of education is to give children skills and knowledge so that they can find employment. Does this mean that education is intended to convert local children into cogs in the economic wheel? This is not a problem in itself but it becomes a problem when they realise that the learning process has not made them capable of introspection and creativity. Therefore, SARVAM has thrown open a menu of opportunities for children to choose from and pick up what interests them. This has been done through academic assistance, encouraging sports and games, art and painting, dance, introduction to computers and animation and so on.

Similarly, the bond between parents, and teachers through regular PTA and VEC meetings served the purpose of making differences vanish and improve relationships in the locality. These meetings initially started with a lot of heated discussions but after explanations from both sides and airing of bottled up feelings, now takes place more cordially. The insensitivity to the point of view of others faded. ***They realised there is nothing in this world that cannot be solved through dialogue and discussion, provided both the parties are willing to listen to each other and be prepared to see things from the other's point of view as well.***

Each one's consciousness got an awakening that they needed to be a little more responsible—as parents and teachers. Bringing local institutions to play their role effectively, and creating the awakening in their consciousness that before pointing fingers at others one needs to listen. If we are busy mentally preparing our reactions to what is being said then we are missing half of communication. This awareness is an enablement provided by SARVAM to look inward into one's ownself, and to learn *deep listening*. SARVAM needed to bring into play such consciousness awakening strategies as well because children grow up watching their parents.

Youth Power: Youth is a source of tremendous potential available in villages. SARVAM has thus used the youngsters, giving them recognition

and responsibilities. Many of the youth remained indifferent to SARVAM activities initially but they started joining hands with SARVAM one by one through friends who were already involved in SARVAM's works. Now, they run supplementary tuition centres, organise sports and games, medical camps and so on. Indeed, they manage the Sathyam centre for village development, which serves as a place where the village children and women can come to read, sit and discuss.

Some of the local youth have started new livelihood ventures with the assistance of SARVAM. Their outlook towards development of individuals, families and communities has changed for the better. After their association with SARVAM, they are able to distinguish 'being rude' from 'being bold'; and 'being intrusive' from 'being inquisitive'. They have given up visiting alcohol shops, and have started thinking about living life with dignity through conscious self-exploration, and self-correction. One can recognize their aspirations and the perseverance that have come about.

Summer Camps: The summer camp activities have demonstrated children's talents to their own parents and to the general public in their villages. They get applause from everyone, which motivates them to go on and do even better, both in studies as well as in sports. In fact, it is the talent & showcasing of children during summer camps that gained SARVAM a good name from the entire community and got parents participating in SARVAM's activities in large numbers. They started thinking seriously about their children's studies and what their children should become in the future. ***The introduction of computers to the school children was another milestone in the success story of these communities that SARVAM works with. Children started exploring the possibilities and drawing animated stories using multi-media software. The progress children made in learning computers was unbelievable. They showed a lot of interest and manifested a whole new level of confidence.***

Rural school children, irrespective of whether they are in government or private schools, began to excel in academics, sports and games, and working with computers, proving that ***all that is needed is a facilitative atmosphere and no fear about making mistakes while learning. A poorly equipped school environment, guarded by a sleepy teacher is certainly not conducive to child development.***

Social Capital: SARVAM has built the social capital through networking and connections, both within the community and outside. The revolving fund arrangement is a kind of social capital built within the community which helps the community to get access to financial capital. SARVAM trains the people, for example, farmers to cultivate fodder for cows, through the expertise available in KVK, and MSSRF (M.S. Swaminathan Research Foundation), which has helped improve the human capital. The improved road facility has provided for physical capital, making for easy access to the town, whether to the market or to a hospital. Thus, ***SARVAM has made systematic intervention to contribute to the social, financial, human, and physical capitals that improve the quality of life of people.***

Never Work at Cross Purposes: In principle, SARVAM intends to complement the efforts of the government, and would never work at cross purposes with the government. But, out of goodness, it has happened in some instances when SARVAM had made financial contributions on behalf of the community to obtain some government schemes. This is something SARVAM has realised should never be repeated. It makes the idea of community contribution a failure, and also creates a kind of dependency syndrome among the villagers.

Local News: The village magazine (*Grama Pudhiya Udhayam*) was a source of news for the local people to know about the complete activities of SARVAM in other places as well. They felt pride when reading their

stories in print as well as to read in print pieces of news written by them. It helped the purpose of adult education, and transparency in development transactions. It may also serve the purpose of documenting a development timeline in the service villages of SARVAM. Thus SARVAM has taken a transformative stance in about sixty of its service villages. SARVAM's approach to development are being replicated in other neighbourhood villages with the blessings of the Divine mother. SARVAM has made it a point not to allow the funds and budget to pose a hurdle in supporting any new initiative that deserves support. The basic tenet is: *begin keeping the Divine Mother in mind. Resources will flow where there is gratitude and trust.*

The lessons we have learnt from SARVAM's experiment in the service villages could be one good source of answers to our question: 'How does development take place?' We have noted how SARVAM chose the villages; what were the entry point activities taken up; how building social infrastructure helped improve the well-being of the people, especially children in the schools; how livelihood activities helped enhance household income levels; how housing helped the poor take on a new lease of life; and how all the efforts of SARVAM resulted in bringing about changes in the quality of life of ordinary people in rural villages. More so, in the process, the noticeable levels of raising self-awareness among the community.

The activities of SARVAM focusing on children, the schools, livelihood diversification, sports and games, summer camps, computer classes etc. have reinforced confidence not only in the children, but also gave a whole new outlook to the way parents view studies and extra-curricular activities. ***SARVAM is surely on the way to improving the quality of life in the service villages taking education for children, and livelihoods diversification of parents as the instrumental means. As a result children in the service villages of SARVAM are coming out with flying colours with good scores from schools and in sports activities. Children brought up in such an environment with constant exposure to progress and goodness tend to imbibe aspirations to live in a better society than what they witness their parents live in.***

Chapter 5

Sustainability and Replication

Introduction

The idea of SARVAM was to test in practice the concept of 'Integral Rural Development' in two villages to start with, and then replicate the lessons to a larger area. SARVAM has extended its works to more than sixty villages as of 2023. The main activities and some of the lessons from this SARVAM experiment were presented in Chapter 4. Some aspects of sustainability and replication are presented in the current chapter. The development approach, methods and principles that emerged from SARVAM's work and how we explain it as spiritual approach to rural development are presented in Chapters 6 & 7.

In this chapter now, we shall look at some aspects of sustainability, and replication of how such tenets got grounded. A sustainable strategy should naturally include SARVAM phasing itself out from the activities of the initial two villages, and taking its programmes to other villages.

We have also conducted certain internal exercises to have a clearer idea of the strengths and weaknesses of the existing SARVAM experiments. We, therefore, begin this chapter with a sustainability analysis exercise. The purpose is to record what we do well and what requires improvement when we scale up, followed by perceptions of responsible well-being.

Team Vision

What We Do Well

- Supplementary Education (evening tuition) enabling children to perform academically well.
- Extra-curricular activities such as sports and games that SARVAM's children win laurels wherever they participate.
- Children's corner that helps build character and nurture multiple talents of children.
- English language proficiency and Computer skills to children.
- Increasing women's awareness—motivation—empowerment process.
- Assistance to the vulnerable and marginalized.
- Digital financial awareness.
- Digital financial transactions.
- SHG organization, periodical meeting, and discuss multifarious topics.
- Every rural woman to hold an active bank account.
- SHG bank linkage.
- Develop network with other institutions such as health care, animal care, eye care etc.
- Entrepreneurship development and livelihoods enhancement.
- Sanitation coverage could be achieved with SBM-G.
- Making the women and children functionally own the SARVAM centre.

What Needs Improvement

- Insufficient assistance for school infrastructure improvement.
- Health care—health card for every household was the plan but not achieved.
- A section of the youth still remains onlookers.
- Household kitchen waste management insufficient.
- Involvement of men in SARVAM's activities is wanting. It has come to be viewed as an institution for women and children.

What We Should Discontinue Doing

- SARVAM making financial contributions to government projects on behalf of the community.

What We Should Start Doing

- Health card for every household.
- Enabling SHG products to reach economies of scale.
- Improvement in packaging and branding of SHG products.
- Exposure of SHG women to other successful women SHGs in the country.
- Focus on organic food cultivation to improve nutritional status of children and families.

What We Should Continue Doing

- Education programme is going well. We need to prepare sustainability plans to continue with this.
- English language proficiency programme is doing well and renders positive results.
- Digital financial transactions and Digital Sakhis become local leaders.
- Activities at Children's Corner are doing well. We need to sustain this.
- The support given to women, the vulnerable and marginalized sections of the community should be continued.
- The nutritious snacks that children get from our centre at Poothurai must continue.
- Promoting nutria-gardens at household level, and enhancing green cover in common areas.

Hopes of Sustainability

- School education has improved in the locality because of SARVAM's interventions such as supplementary tuition classes and children's corner. Batch after batch students who attended supplementary couching at SARVAM score high marks in Higher Secondary level examinations. The parents are motivated and observe the growth and behaviour of their children.

- Consistently after SARVAM's intervention, the number of students who go into science stream is on the increase, which is an indication that their academic performance is getting better.
- Women are active in whatever livelihood activities they opted for. With little guidance and distant overseeing, all the livelihood programmes can go on.
- With regard to Health—be it general health check-up, or eye-care, or animal care—SARVAM conducts periodical camps. However, the benefits of Government of India's National Rural Health Mission require to be tapped.
- After the launch of the SBM-G in 2014 toilet construction in all the houses reached saturation. After the launch of Jal Jeevan Mission in 2019, the Government of Tamil Nadu and Government of Puducherry are providing tap connections to all the rural households. Thus, water and sanitation related problems have been, to a large extent, addressed. However, the problem of solid waste and wastewater require to be addressed.
- Growing organic foods which was part of the original plan of SARVAM is yet to take off at the scale expected. However, nutrition gardens have been promoted. They are spreading in all the houses.
- The Dairy Cooperative is already working independently.
- The Women Community Fund is already working independently.
- Parent-Teacher Associations in schools are active and they have the capability to carry on.
- Some local youths have become able to manage the tuition centres. They can even run tuition centres commercially.
- The health camps introduced them various hospitals and veterinary clinics. People have come in touch with many hospitals, so with their increased awareness they can take care of their health.
- The bank linkage is very strong. Digital transactions are admirably well. Women are in touch with banks for their financial dealings. The operation of moneylenders have considerably come down.
- School children attending Children's Corner and tuition centres talk and behave very responsibly and are willing to share work and take responsibility.
- The employment opportunities in the vicinity of villages have grown significantly. The youth are engaged, and earning.

Status of various sectors of Intervention/Institutions				
Sector/Institution	*Status*			*Remarks*
	Thriving	*Struggling*	*Suffering*	
1. EDUCATION	☼			**Overall it is thriving**
1.1 Supplementary coaching	☼			Doing well. It has become an awaited event. It requires continuing support for some time.
1.2 Support to govt. schools	☼			
1.3 Computer Classes	☼			
1.4 Children's Corner	☼			
1.5 English Access Programme	☼			
2. HEALTH CARE				
2.1 Health awareness	☼			This stands half-done.
2.2 Access to medical services	☼			
2.3 Integral health	☼			
2.4 Health Card				
2.5 Health Insurance		😐		Health camps are regular.
2.6 Health Camps	☼			
3. DRINKING WATER				
3.1 Access to drinking water	☼	😐		This is being fulfilled by the Jal Jeevan Mission of the Govt. of India in all the TN villages.
3.2 Adequacy of water	☼			
3.3 Safety of water	☼			
3.4 Awareness on water handling				
4. SANITATION				The SBM-G has been made use of to complete this task in household and schools.
4.1 Sanitation culture	☼		😐	
4.2 Access to sanitation	☼			
4.3 Use and maintenance	☼			
4.4 Household waste disposal				
5. HOUSING				
5.1 Occupancy	☼			

(*Contd.*)

Sector/Institution	*Status*			*Remarks*
	Thriving	*Struggling*	*Suffering*	
5.2 Maintenance	☼			
6. LIVELIHOODS				
6.1 Diversified Activities	☼			
6.2 Accounting discipline	☼			
6.3 Loan repayment	☼			
6.4 Entrepreneurship training				
6.5 Entrepreneurship activities				
7. COMMUNITY FUND				
7.1 Operational procedures	☼			Well understood
7.2 Repayment status	☼			Satisfactory
7.3 Bank linkage				
7.4 Bank support				
7.5 Digital awareness				
7.6 Digital financial transactions				
8. SUPPORT TO THE ULTRA-POOR				
8.1 Identification of families	☼			
8.2 Activities taken up	☼			
9. COMMUNITY MAGAZINE				
9.1 Content development	☼			
9.2 Printing	☼			
9.3 Circulation	☼			
10. SHARANAM—CSRT				
10.1 Training facility				
10.2 Research has to take off				
10.3 A great facility in use by SARVAM and other development organisations				

Note: Thriving means strong, consistent, and progressing. It is likely to go on even if we phase out; Struggling means moderate or inconsistent. It may thrive with a little support for some time; Suffering means it is at high risk of not continuing without outside help.

Many private companies have come up in the vicinity of Pondicherry and Villupuram. These places have become a source of employment for men, women and youth. They realize their commitments and are on the lookout for opportunities they can grab. Most of them have become earning members in their families. They can carry on by themselves. As they gain experience their wages keep improving or they keep shifting from one company to another with a view to getting higher pay. They also come to SARVAM to have their skills further honed so that they become easily employable, or their wages get enhanced. This is to say that besides promoting local entrepreneurs, SARVAM also supports—with skill development training—those willing to go out in search of semi-skilled and skilled employment.

Active Play—Experiences of SARVAM

Children need a healthy balance of high-energy active play like running, jumping, skipping as well as passive play like sitting in front of a chess board or carrom board. ***Children spend many hours each day in the care of teachers, so providing the recommended amount of active play is important in helping children establish healthy habits.***

Development through physical play has been an integral part of the work being done in the SARVAM villages. This enables children to achieve their maximum potential by focusing on holistic overall development using physical activities and games. This is essentially about getting kids running and playing, which activate physical growth and mental alertness. During the Daily Activities Corner emphasis is placed on physical activities and games, where they play volley ball, throw ball, athletics, and perform classical dance, karate and so on.

Everyday about 400 children come into the Community Centres and play various games as part of their overall development. A Summer Camp is organized every year for the children when they have their mid-summer break. The camp consists of boys and girls between the ages of 5 to 16. At the camp children choose a particular play activity according to their likes—dancing, singing, drama, sports, painting, handicraft etc. They are given special classes to develop these talents. During the camp, special games and sports sessions are conducted for the children helping them to learn, grow, communicate and develop as confident individuals. The success SARVAM witnessed in this activity requires furthering.

SARVAM would like to further these efforts and develop a round-the-year programme that seeks to build physical, social and personal skills, i.e. holistic development using games and play. The programme aimed at covering 750 children between the ages of 5 and 17 years and was done in collaboration with the Magic Bus (http:// www.magicbus.org) which has pioneered an Activity Based Curriculum (ABC) that uses games to make change.

Consolidation

Local institution building and capacity building as strategies for local people to take over sustaining the activities have been successfully grounded. All the activities in terms of 'functions' can be taken up by women and children collectively. In recent times—be it organizing supplementary tuition classes, or summer camps—they are spearheaded by local youth and women only. They need to be trained in resource mobilization also. Similarly, the entrepreneurship activities are carried out by women with financial transactions they have either with the groups or with banks they have been linked to. SARVAM initiates only new and refresher training programmes, or takes up review and suggestive meetings. There is also constant motivational/inspirational talks arranged, which are required as energizers to keep the tempo going.

One must participate and witness the annual summer camps to be able to understand who plans, who executes, and who makes the entire camp a success. The locals take over the entire responsibility on themselves as teams. The children take over a portion of the tasks as theirs.

The older children guide and mentor the younger ones. If a younger child tossed a chocolate wrapper by mistake, the older ones do not mind taking it to the dustbin. If a child finds his/her classroom requires cleaning up they assume responsibility and start action. They need not be told by anyone from SARVAM. The order in which the children (and women) leave their footwear outside classrooms has been observed and appreciated by many visitors. There is no such rule that SARVAM imposes, nor is there any penalty if someone tossed a chocolate wrapper, wasted food, or leave their footwear in disarray. Perhaps, that comes as part of the Mother's blessings when someone gets associated with SARVAM activities. They imbibe these habits—habits of responsible well-being after they attend a few sessions and observe the new personal norms being followed by everyone as normal day-to-day.

The Idea of 'Responsible Well-being'

SARVAM is operationalizing the idea of Responsible well-being, through various activities. The activities listed above might—on the surface—look like simple education activities or SHG and bank linkage activities. The approach adopted by SARVAM in operationalizing and the process followed are deliberate in order to ensure that the implicit purpose, and the associated interactions result in self-awareness. There are many specific activities such as cultural tour programme, joint prayer etc. that serve consolidating such purpose. The overall perceived well-being of women, children and families in general has been captured through various indicators. They are presented below.

Network and Official Connections: The social capital and official connections that the people of Poothurai and Perambai have made in the course of the Village Development Project being implemented by SARVAM is commendable. Those village leaders who took active part in the activities of SARVAM must have discovered social and official connections can take their villages to great heights, provided they use these connections honestly for social development causes. They are in touch with many departments of the government; many government officials know that these two villages are model villages established with the assistance of SARVAM; the community members are in touch with several hospitals; and staff from these hospitals go to these villages to hold periodical health camps; the community members have been introduced to insurance companies of repute and many of them now have life and health insurance cover, to mention just a few benefits. If the community leaders are smart enough, they should be able to make the benefits sustain long after SARVAM phasing out.

Capacity Building: SARVAM takes up capacity building of the existing institutions. The Village Panchayats functionaries, Youth Club members, Women Self-help Group leaders, and active members of the PTA have to be orientated and trained to take over. The members of the Housing Committee, for instance, have participated and witnessed for themselves how to allot housing to the needy and deserving. They have undergone practical training on how to apply local criteria to identify the poorest of the poor amongst communities where many families are poor; the youth have taken active part in conducting annual Summer Camps. With systematically planned training and capacity building these community groups and institutions should be able to take over and manage activities in their community.

An attendant question is: Are they willing to take over? Capacity building training of the community groups or Panchayats to take over should include preparing the mental make-up of the community too. That is part of 'responsible well-being', which is one of the core elements of the Village Development Project. That is the reason we are going for a gradual phase out rather than abrupt withdrawal.

Strategy Followed in Sustainability

Four-pronged activities were undertaken in the SARVAM villages for sustaining the activities. They are:

- **Consolidation:** First of all, a fresh set of activities with a view to filling any gaps in the achievements made so far. These are gaps identified through the Cantrill's Self-anchoring Ladder, e.g. Integral Health, water, sanitation etc.
- **Phase-out:** Secondly, institution and capacity building activities were taken up as part of the phase-out plan.
- **New Projects:** Thirdly, SARVAM took up many new projects supported by HDFC, L&T FS, US Embassy etc. in order to consolidate and to spread to new villages. They included English language programme, Financial Literacy and Digital Transactions, Entrepreneurship development etc.
- **Spreading Out:** Fourthly, SARVAM worked with fresh plans in a set of new villages replicating the methods adopted in the first two villages, viz. Poothurai and Perambai.

Nutrition Education and Growing Organic Foods—Experience of SARVAM

Nutrition education and growing fresh foods is about enabling access to fresh vegetables and fruits to rural households. Health and well-being have a strong connection with generating physical energy to perform the day's work and a state of mind that is active. ***Rural people have the habit of filling the stomach to be relieved of hunger rather than providing for the nutritional requirements of their body. The sense of daily nutritional in-take from what one eats is absolutely absent, irrespective of whether one is an expectant mother, or breast-feeding mother, or an elderly person.*** Making informed food choices and preparing healthy snacks are part of integral health. Nutri-gardens promoted during the SARVAM's Village Development Project provided 'a sense of nutrition from household vegetables and fruits, without having to spend extra money'.

Working with expert volunteers and accessing government awareness programmes, the project team has been creating awareness on the various aspects of maintaining good health, nutrition and hygiene. These programmes have been instrumental in raising the awareness of people regarding organic food, nutritional value of various locally available vegetables, fruits, egg and milk.

SARVAM subsequently sought to create a fundamental change in the areas of Nutrition and Health, and thus making it a model for all the service villages to emulate.

Growing Organic Foods

The project team introduced organic farming for developing community gardens and individual nutri-gardens. Villagers can grow their own fresh foods that help them address the challenges of malnutrition and preventing anaemia. A 3.5 acre piece of land, adjacent to the SARVAM community centre, was developed as an experimental plot for community garden. It was used as a school of practice to learn the basics of organic farming and get the necessary support to maintain their own nutria-gardens. Making use of group loans as well as support from institutions such as NABARD, the community members pursue promoting sustainable agricultural practices, and nutria-gardens.

Over the years, the villagers along with the project team collaborated with NSS volunteers to plant trees in an endeavour towards creating a green environment that can mitigate climate change disasters, while at the same time become conducive to the enhancement of health and hygiene.

Spread Out Strategy

Replication and scaling up of SARVAM's experiments beyond Poothruai and Perambai has been an important aspect of the development agenda of the Village Development Project. With a view to making it a reality in October 2013 SARVAM conducted a rapid rural appraisal (RRA) in 12 Village Panchayats in two blocks, Vanur and Vikravandi, of Villupuram district, Tamil Nadu. This RRA aimed at collecting base-line information, and participatory problem identification in each of the 12 VPs. The total population in these 12 VPs is 24,500, making up 7150 households. As planned it was extended to 12 Village Panchayats initially. Later on, it has been extended to about 60 villages.

The SARVAM Ripple

The ripple SARVAM aims at causing is very simple, as you could have noticed. All that is required is reflective rural development practitioners, who are observant more of the process. SARVAM replicated its model, initially in 12 Village Panchayats, and now it is spread in about 60 villages. One of the vital contributions of SARVAM's Village Development Project to rural development literature in terms of rural development practice is: ***Activities with children can make best entry point for any rural development activity introduced from outside; then move on to their mothers (women), then the youths naturally tend to become inquisitive. The circle goes on expanding.*** Once on the go, all that is required to be done is to make sure that those coming into the circle are really poor and deserve assistance. We will go with this approach. This is being replicated in all the service villages of SARVAM at the moment.

The formula adopted in designing intervention activities start with children, as in Set-1 below, and then moves on to Set-2, and Set-3.

Set-1

- **Anganwadis:** Support and improve the local Child Care Centres (quality of care plus infrastructure).
- **Active Play:** Introduce Active Play and nutritional supplements in anganwadis and schools.
- **Supplementary education** to school children to improve the performance of children in government-run primary and high schools.
- **Computer classes** that build confidence and offer equality of exposure to rural children.
- **Summer Camps:** Organise summer camps that unite and demonstrate the talents of rural children besides teaching responsibility sharing.

Set-2

- **Women Livelihoods:** Bring diversity in rural livelihoods so as to improve household income.

- **Community Revolving Fund:** It dramatically improves cash flow in rural households, and prevents the rural poor from falling into the clutches of professional moneylenders.

Set-3

- **Youth Leadership:** Motivating and positively charging rural youth to become transformative, responsible local leaders.
- **Digital Financial Literacy:** Despite rural backgrounds, digital financial literacy has enabled people to use technology. This has provided access to financial services such as banking, loans, and insurance, which were previously unavailable. It has also enabled those living in rural areas to participate in the global economy, which has led to increased economic stability and growth.

Centre for Sustainable Rural Transformation

SHARANAM—Centre for Sustainable Rural Transformation is a launch-pad for disseminating the successful rural transformation practices reported by SARVAM. SARVAM is a social laboratory that passes on success stories and best practices to Sharanam for dissemination. Precisely, SARVAM is a field-lab, and Sharanam is primarily a training-*cum*-research centre. Thus, SARVAM and Sharanam are two sides of the same coin, working in tandem and learning from each other.

SARVAM has been in existence for about two decades now. It has demonstrated in practice 'Integral Rural Development'. The experiences have been documented and the results are encouraging. We are taking the lessons learnt to larger and larger groups of communities in the State of Tamil Nadu. SARVAM is working in sixty villages currently as of 2023. Now with the support of Sharanam, SARVAM's work will spread larger and faster.

Development Outlook

Sharanam envisions having a broader development outlook rather than merely being a training centre. Sharanam is a centre for training, research and extension in 'Integral Rural Development', which is the bottom line both for SARVAM and Sharanam. ***That means development that transcends socio-economic well-being of individuals and goes further to touch upon the consciousness of a person, and thus of a community,***

to enable them lead a life that an individual values the most giving shape to inner-self.

It is a kind of human-spirit-centred approach to bring about a systemic change in the way one perceives change and improvement in the quality of life. SARVAM or Sharanam has not introduced any religious reading into this concept of rural development. Since the approach is systemic it essentially cuts across the sector-specific boundaries of development to bring about 'rural transformation'. Sharanam looks at development solutions through 'sustainability' lens.

The conventional 'Integrated Rural Development' is sector-specific and materialistic, and has very little to do with the consciousness or inner-self of the community members. ***Rural development in the generally understood sense of the term goes around making carbon copies of urban life, with facility improvement as the focus. If rural transformation has to take place, one needs to go beyond the sector boundaries within which development is often discussed and understood.*** The word 'integrated' goes with the concept of development; whereas 'integral' goes with the concept of transformational change. In Integral Rural Development, the 'process' assumes primacy and the materialistic delivery of certain facilities are incidental or attendant. In other words, training or provision of basic common facilities aimed at nurturing the human mind on right/wrong discrimination—both on consciousness and material well-being. This is education/awareness on the practice of 'responsible well-being', which contributes to/results in sustainability. ***This requires constant development research as well, because bringing about 'transformational change' is more challenging and time consuming than 'development' that aims at target-based outcome and is time-bound.***

Many development organizations 'do the same thing and expect different results'. If the product you want to offer is different, necessarily your recipe or the process of making has to be different. Sharanam believes that quality of life is as important as standard of living. Quality of life has more to do with inner-self or consciousness of individuals and communities, whereas standard of living is narrowly economic in sense. That means it is not merely social infrastructure and the economic means to achieve a desired standard of living but that the process of development has to incorporate development ethics, values, and being able to discriminate on sustainable solutions from low-cost ones that are unsustainable. Sharanam is very much conscious of 'the means to achieve the transformative change—that must be human-spirit-centred and sustainable'. This is the development outlook that singles out Sharanam from other organisations we generally come across in the name of development today.

It is not merely achieving certain desirable development targets by providing better social infrastructure or facilities to make life easier. It is bringing about change in the people through a process of self-awakening in order to enable them—(i) realize their potentials and achieve what they value most in life; and (ii) be able to discriminate both on mental consciousness and material well-being. This makes Sharanam outstanding and relevant in its approach to addressing the contemporary issues of development and under-development.

The Vision

A strong, enlightened, prosperous and progressive India—a leader in the ways of spirituality, a friend and helper of all the people.

The Mission

- Initiate a movement for an integral village development which aims at establishing and developing a progressive and happy village community, empowered and directed from within, and is based on a new consciousness and values.
- Integrate and try to bring harmony and perfection in every aspect of village life, based on a spiritual approach.
- Help every individual of the village community, with no divisions of age, gender, caste or religion, to realize his/her highest physical, emotional, mental and spiritual potential.
- Create iconic rural leaders known as 'Transformative Leaders' by imparting knowledge through constant orientation, training programmes, and capacity building exercises.

Guiding Principles and Values

- **Collaborate and Complement:** Work in order to complement the efforts of the regional governments, Local NGOs and international development agencies, and be alert never to work at cross-purposes.
- **Sustainable and Cost-Effective Technologies:** Opt and advocate for the use of suitable and sustainable technologies that are cost-

effective and of high quality, rather than low cost technologies that produce low quality results.

- **Recognize Your Agents of Rural Transformation:** Recognize that the most powerful agents of rural transformation are the women, youth and children. They need to play a central role and have to be prepared to take up responsibilities.
- **Promote Harmony and Peace:** Encourage all types of activities which lead to bonding, relationships, a feeling of harmony, helpfulness and oneness within the village, with the surrounding villages and with the country as a whole.
- **Believe in the Divine Presence:** We believe that we are not just the body, the emotions or the thoughts, though they all play a very important role in our lives. We have within us another dimension which has been called by various names—the Soul, the Spirit, the Divine Presence. It is the source of all harmony, unity, love, compassion and beauty, naturally and spontaneously. It is this which has to be helped to come forward in ourselves and in the village community, and to manifest in every field and activity.

Strategic Direction

The Scale of Operations

Sharanam—CSRT has an ambitious scale of becoming a global centre for training, research and dissemination of best practices. The potentials visualized are enormous and the possibilities are endless. But, primarily this training centre belongs to grassroots level leaders in India. As the works expand, the scale of operation of Sharanam will also keep expanding to cover South Asian, Asian, African countries, including the developed countries that have come to believe in integral development, ethics in development, and sustainable development.

Scope of Programmes

- Local and Regional Development.
- Civil Society Engagement.
- Basic Service Delivery.
- Livelihoods Diversification.
- Vocational Education and Training.
- Transformational Change.

- Development Research.
- Development Communication and Training.
- Environment, Sustainability and Development.
- Climate–Resilient Development.

Range of Stakeholders

- Men, women and youth from the rural areas.
- Like-minded NGOs.
- Women Self-help Group Leaders.
- Traditional Leaders from Community groups.
- Potential Youth leaders.
- Elected Panchayat representatives.
- School Teachers.
- Social Activists.
- Members of Community based Organisations.
- Micro Entrepreneurs.
- Government machinery at the grassroots and programme planning levels.
- University and College teachers.
- Development funding agencies.

Thematic Focus and Goals

Theme 1: Education, Training and Capacity Building

- **GOAL 1:** Enhance human capabilities as a credible strategy for rural transformation to take place. Education and training in vocational skills shall form part of individual capacity building.
- **GOAL 2:** Taking up capacity building exercises and actions that diversify rural livelihoods as a means to do away with the inheritance of poverty in rural areas.

Theme 2: Grassroots Leadership Development

- **GOAL 1:** Leadership development for elected representatives of local bodies, especially Village Panchayats. There are also prospective youth leaders whose positive energy remains untapped and who have the potential to become transformative leaders. They shall be nurtured for the common good, and CSRT will provide the mentoring.

- **GOAL 2:** Democracy works best where the citizens are responsible and responsive. Developing active citizens/responsible citizens will also be an important goal in leadership development as it will help develop a vision for the individual and for the community.

Theme 3: Institution Development

- **GOAL 1:** Develop appropriate local institutions vital for the transformational process to get local grounding, and sustenance. These can be social institutions like self-help groups; economic institutions like banks or cooperatives; educational institutions like schools; and political institutions like Village Panchayats. CSRT will identify the needs for the creation of such new institutions and enhance the capacity of existing institutions.
- **GOAL 2:** Renew, enliven and rebuild the capacity of existing local institutions and build support for their connectedness. Sharanam shall actively play the connector and help build support for their connection to outside institutions that could be useful to the community.

Theme 4: Development Research

- **GOAL 1:** Carry out research on grassroots level issues as part of the regular work of Sharanam. It can range from policy research to action-research to impact analysis of government schemes.
- **GOAL 2:** Serve as a training ground for young development researchers and research-minded development practitioners to improve their skills of studying and reporting grassroots level issues.

Theme 5: Development Communication

- **GOAL 1:** Take up activities that empower people through information and public education as a means for rural transformation. CSRT shall prepare training modules, booklets, leaflets, DVDs, etc. for educational/training purposes. They will be in different languages for dissemination to a wide variety of the target community.
- **GOAL 2:** Organise and provide a platform for conducting national and international level seminars and conferences on issues of development, underdevelopment and sustainability.

Theme 6: Programme Exploration

- **GOAL 1:** Explore the practicability of innovative ideas, approaches and strategies in sustainable development tried elsewhere.
- **GOAL 2:** Creation or early development of pilot projects that break new ground in support of transformational change objectives. Start creative and innovative community projects.

Theme 7: Programme Demonstration and Scaling

- **GOAL 1:** Showing how pilot projects can be replicated, or promoting the scaling-up of such projects to a larger geographical area.
- **GOAL 2:** Demonstrating what works best at various levels—such as in one village, in a cluster of villages, in a region, in a country and so on.

Theme 8: Inclusive Development

- **GOAL 1:** To bring about inclusive development so as to make social guarantees a reality. Applying social guarantee laws and rights based policies to work in favour of inclusion and creating opportunities for the poor.
- **GOAL 2:** The other goal here is combating corruption and demanding transparent development administration in service delivery for the poor. Taking up programmes and joining hands to align with those who work towards inclusive development and fight against corruption by whatever means.

Theme 9: Development Sadhanas

- **GOAL 1:** Develop a mindset to instil faith in peace and harmony; respect nature rather than try to conquer it; have faith in sustainable solutions rather than instant ones; cultivate a mind that respects values and principles in human living rather than gaining power over others, which is brutal in mindset and lives by the law of the jungle.
- **GOAL 2:** Offer development *Sadhanas* for everyone—children, youth, women, traditional and elected leaders of rural villages, householders, the physically challenged and so on. Help them to practice conscious awareness.

Theme 10: Development Consultancy

- **GOAL 1:** Offer development consultancy by undertaking sponsored research studies, documentation, programme planning exercises, and professional development exercises, and guide corporate houses write CSR Policy and 'meaningful giving' programmes etc.
- **GOAL 2:** Extend cooperation and work in close collaboration with any organization that supports community stewardship, promotes green technologies and a viable future for humans.

Approaches and Strategies

- Stakeholder Development and Collaboration.
- Network Development and Convening.
- Capacity Building and Technical Assistance.
- Programmatic/Sector-wide Approach.
- Institution Building and Strengthening.
- Promoting Green Technologies.
- Advocacy and Campaigns.
- Effective use of media (including the Internet).

Mission

- Establish the fundamentals required in order to take up programmes (training, development research, publications, stakeholder development and collaborations etc.) for making Sharanam get off the ground as a centre for sustainable solutions.
- Demonstrate innovations in development practices brought out by SARVAM on a larger scale.
- Research on basic service delivery gaps (education, health care, water and sanitation, rural housing, and household energy consumption) and find mechanisms to bridge the service delivery gaps.
- Opportunities brought about by liberalization and privatization are aplenty. But, the rural youth have to be prepared to grab those opportunities through skills development and livelihoods diversification programmes.
- The 'total absence of conscious awareness' has resulted in extensive damage to trees, water bodies and rural livelihoods. People

have to regain their conscience so that planet earth shall have environmental recovery.

- Build grassroots level leadership (Youth Transformative Leaders) and local institution building exercises through stakeholder development and collaboration with the idea of achieving good governance, and grassroots level democracy.
- Get down to doing programme exploration so as to (i) communicate development *sadhanas*; (ii) address issues of inequality and inheritance of poverty; and (iii) take the flight direction towards achieving sustainable rural transformation.

Chapter 6

Transformations & Responsible Well-being

The operational methodology adopted by SARVAM flows like the rainwater running down stream with simple gravitational force. It's the gravity that enables the flow happen is intuitively understandable to your scientific mind, although you cannot notice gravity as such. The same holds good for SARVAM's method of working with children and families in this part of the country. The development strategy adopted was locally grounded, but universally applicable. This section goes to explain how this transformation happens.

The approach entails: Begin with children keeping in view the end in mind that you are going to impact on the entire family. Believe that *every child is a promise.* That promise can be turned into a great self-propelling force even without the child knowing it. They are the ones who are going to become transformative leaders in the future. All that is required is discovering the power of the promise; appropriate coaching and mentoring; enabling the parents of that child to recognize what this boy or girl loves doing, which the world needs. Just be available to that child. Don't just hand them any rules. Simply ask them purposeful questions that have profound meaning underneath. Let them explore, have fun, watch, observe and learn anything in a playful way.

Awareness and Self-discovery: Awareness comes through self-discovery. Self-discovery happens when right questions are asked. The strategy to find the right answer is: 'asking the right questions in the first place'. Not by giving ready answers. This means that when one is taken deeper and deeper inside an issue—asking the right

M. Nargesh Banu D/o Mohammed Ibrahim, B.A. English, Nesal, 23 years

I am Nargeshbanu from a poor Muslim family. My parents did not want to send me to college. The reason—I am a girl, and particularly from a minority community. But ever since I attended English classes in SARVAM, I nurtured a dream of becoming an English teacher. I was disheartened and remained confused, when my parents asked me to discontinue my studies. Incidentally, my mother attended an awareness programme conducted by SARVAM on Women Education. Then she could convince my father. They allowed me to join in a community college, where the fees were very nominal. I approached SARVAM seeking help for my educational attainments, which every time I got. I got scholarship to continue my studies. Now I am happy because I am doing my Under Graduate degree in B.A. English. I am really grateful to SARVAM for they made my dream come to true. I believe the secret now that if we deeply desire, and if our prayers are true, God will conjure ways to make it possible. Prayer in fact is repeated chanting of what we aspire in life.

questions—he/she progressively moves to a state of self-awareness leading to clarity of thought and clarity in decision making. It is more through self-search; introspection; and careful observation of interactions of man with the society and nature, during his day-to-day livelihood engagements. This is about expanding one's perceptual ability. They discover how the world works; how to distinguish morality from immorality; what does it mean to be ethical or unethical; how some societies are developed, while others are not, and so on and so forth. SARVAM is very conscious about making sure that this happens.

There is nothing stern: This is not done as a stern or painstaking exercise. At SARVAM, children learn lessons through play, songs, drawing and painting, gymnastics, games and conversations. The annual summer camp is the most enjoyed activity-series for children, where specialists working in the sphere of 'child development' come to interact and learn. The experts arrive with their accumulated knowledge on psychology, and skill-sets to work with children on creative activities. At the end of the camp, they have always remarked that they learnt much more from the children than what they believe to have made the children learn.

For instance, SARVAM took up an experiment in digital financial literacy for women. Many rural women own a smartphone. They generally use the phone either to call her husband or another SHG member. Beyond that, two other uses known to them were using the in-built camera and at times to check WhatsApp. The Digital Sakhi Programme aimed at imparting digital financial literacy. Women found it a little difficult to pick up partly because they are not used to experimenting with phones, and mostly because they were afraid that a wrong click may result in their hard earned money to get washed away to some unknown destination. But the reality is that the physical environment they live in has moved to using smart phones. Thus, they cannot choose to be left behind. This will otherwise mean allowing them to remain cut away from the contemporariness. Something needed to be done.

The trainer came to know, through a casual conversation, that children in those families are too interested in using smart phone. That they stealthily do all kinds of experiments with mobile phones; that they understand the smartphones inside out. The trainer who came to know about it, asked the women, if they have any objection in bringing their children also to attend Digital Literacy Programmes on Saturdays and Sundays. Children came along with their mothers. They were just allowed to sit with the mothers who were attending the training. No instructions given to the children.

The children were watching, what was going on. They could not hold themselves when they found their mothers fumbling and groping not understanding the instructions given by the trainer. The children gradually started prodding their teaching mothers what instructions were being given by the trainer. So, sitting next to their mother every child started teaching their mothers how to use smartphone for transacting money safely using digital platforms. It was learnt later that a kind of reverse homeschooling also took place at home—the child teaching the mother at home, whenever the mother was in doubt in digital transactions using mobile phone. This is just one. There are many more to narrate how learning takes place, or how development takes place—physical and mental.

Watching is not observing: Children observe and learn more, than what they are taught formally in the closed environment of a classroom. They grow up observing (not merely watching) how their parents transact with each other; how they transact with the neighbours or with the larger society. Observation is about involvement or intense engagement.

Children observe where their parents keep an *intimate distance*, where they keep *personal distance*; where they maintain a *social distance*; and the things they completely *distance away* from. What goes with the prevailing social norms and what goes with personal norm of their parents etc. They subconsciously get to differentiate the intimate from the personal and the social. This observation and socialization process helps firming up their personal norms, character *vis-à-vis* the prevailing social norms. The activities of SARVAM meant for the children and women [mothers] subtly nurture such interactions—at times through deliberately designed experiments such as making the children sit next to their mothers in the training programmes on mobile-based digital transactions.

Responsible well-being: In order for the child to progress mentally or towards realizing her promise, the parents have to essentially watch the dialogue at home—be it between the husband and wife; or as parents with the children. A community cultivated like this, and a whole neighbourhood nurtured like this leads to emergence of a society where one can witness: 'Responsible well-being'.

As mentioned in the previous version, for us [the authors] also it was equally exciting to write about it for two reasons. They are: providing a spiritual perspective to rural development and the approach entails realizing rural development that is human-spirit-centric, rather than narrowing it down to income enhancement and thus poverty reduction. This is not to brush aside the materialistic or welfare needs of a community. Rather it is not about welfare-orientation. It is about self-propulsion. It is about permanence. It is about sustainability. It is about raising the level of self-awareness leading to clarity of decision-making in one's personal life and for the society.

This is because poverty reduction or rural development for that matter is not all about income enhancement, although incomes do find place as a vital element to it. The ultimate purpose of development is human well-being and improving the quality of life of people, and a society that respects responsible well-being. The relationship between the personal and social is vital here. The psychology of personal or simply the human nature is such that it does not want to compromise for the social.

Consciousness Pointer: It is here it becomes significant for us to raise the level of consciousness. It helps activate clarity of thought and enables right decision making. The pointer emphasized in SARVAM experiments is: *whose suffering does it help eliminate? And what's the suffering the person* *endures; and what's the suffering the society endures?* This question must point the person towards the right decision.

Conceptually, the term 'well-being' is used more when we speak at the level of individuals, and quality of life (QoL) somewhat more when we speak of communities, localities, and societies. Similarly, 'well-being' is used somewhat more to refer to actual experience, and quality of life more to refer to context and environments. At times, its well-being might sound more subjective, whereas quality of life is objectively measurable indicators oriented. In this sense, well-being is to do with subjective-well-being and self-assessed state of being. We carried out a simple exercise to have a sense of self-perceived state of well-being or ill-being among the adults involved in the activities of SARVAM. The survey results are presented in the table below.

Perceived Well-being

Sl. No.	Points of Analysis & Reflection	VS Disagree	S Disagree	Agree	S Agree	VS Agree
1.	I am always optimistic about my future	0	0	0	0	101
2.	There have been times when I felt inferior to most of the people, I knew	0	0	0	22	79
3.	My physical health has restricted me in the past	0	1	23	36	41
4.	I believe there is a real purpose for my life	0	0	0	78	23
5.	I will always seek out activities that challenge me to think and reason	0	0	0	99	2
6.	I rarely count on good things happening to me	95	5	1	0	0
7.	In general, I feel confident about my abilities	0	0	1	31	69

(*Contd.*)

Sl. No.	Points of Analysis & Reflection	VS Disagree	S Disagree	Agree	S Agree	VS Agree
8.	Sometimes I wonder if my family will really be there for me when I am in need	63	11	26	1	0
9.	My body seems to resist physical illness very well	0	0	0	27	74
10.	Life does not hold much future promise for me	68	26	7	0	0
11.	I avoid activities which require me to concentrate	93	8	0	0	0
12.	I always look on the bright side of things	0	0	3	22	76
13.	I sometimes think I am a worthless individual	92	8	1	0	0
14.	My friends know they can always confide in me and ask me for advice	0	0	4	36	61
15.	My physical health is excellent	0	0	2	41	58
16.	Sometimes I don't understand what life is all about	0	0	0	20	81
17.	Generally, I feel pleased with the amount of intellectual stimulation I receive in my daily life	0	0	1	17	83
18.	In the past, I have expected the best	0	0	16	85	0

(*Contd.*)

Sl. No.	Points of Analysis & Reflection	VS Disagree	S Disagree	Agree	S Agree	VS Agree
19.	I am uncertain about my ability to do things well in the future	70	3	27	0	1
20.	My family has been available to support me in the past	0	87	14	0	0
21.	I feel a sense of mission about my future	0	0	0	13	88
22.	The amount of information that I process in a typical day is just about right for me (not too much; not too little)	0	0	1	12	88
23.	In the past, I hardly ever expected things to go my way	16	83	1	1	0
24.	I will always be secure with who I am	1	0	0	25	75
25.	In the past, I have not always had friends with whom I could share my joys and sorrows	0	51	47	2	1
26.	In the past, I have generally found intellectual challenges to be vital to my overall well-being	0	0	3	24	74
27.	In the past, I have felt sure of myself among strangers	0	0	0	16	85

(Contd.)

Sl. No.	Points of Analysis & Reflection	VS Disagree	S Disagree	Agree	S Agree	VS Agree
28.	My friends will be there for me when I need help	0	0	0	76	25
29.	I expect my physical health to get worse	98	2	0	1	0
30.	It seems that my life has always had purpose	100	1	0	0	0
31.	My life has often seemed void of positive mental stimulation	101	0	0	0	0

The points of enquiry could be categorized into physical self, emotional self, mental or intellectual self, familial, and social interaction related dimensions of life. It can be read like this.

The Survey Results: The respondents [adults in the service area of SARVAM] are found to be generally optimistic about life, have the attitude of seeing the brighter side of things, and had a feeling they had a purpose in life. Health has never been a restricting factor. They have a tendency to count on the 'good things' that happen in their life.

There was never an occasion, when they felt they are worthless. They are confident and certain about their ability to do better in the future. However, they seem to be slightly wary of their family's support in their endeavours. Sometimes, they tend to ask what life is all about. In the past, they have not always had friends with whom they could share their joys and sorrows. But, the SARVAM association has given a feeling that they have friends whom they can share and seek support/help. The optimism they have learnt through their association with SARVAM can be termed as 'learnt optimism or acquired optimism' that serves as the leading light.

They strongly disagree to the statement that if they thought their life has often seemed void of positive mental stimulation. The amount of intellectual stimulation they get in a day; the physical and mental engagement they keep them busy makes them think they have a mission in life. This is what we deduce from their responses to a series of questions on self-perceived well-being. They have sort of learnt optimism towards life. They are active both physically and mentally, despite the fact that some of them are in their forties and fifties.

The Psychic-being: In Sri Aurobindo's language, it is evolving to achieve supramental consciousness. In his illustration of human development—if we may call so—there is a concentric system that starts by touching the outer being and the physical self of a person, and moving on to impact on the mental and psychic-being. The former can be equated to welfare and utility maximization including income enhancement, whereas the latter can be taken to mean subjective well-being, self-assessed happiness, and enhanced level of responsible well-being.

His message of world unity and human progress was on the basis of a dynamic integration of both material and spiritual values. He further believed that the advent of the Superman is not a far-off divine event, but an imminent goal of evolution. The vision of the evolution of Man into the Superman or the out-flowering of the Divine is in the collective life of humanity. In order to understand it, we need to move beyond the survival

Vanisri, T., Poothurai, 23 years

I live in a remote village at the outskirts of Pondicherry. I am a first generation graduate in my family. My parents have done only their basic schooling. I studied in a Government school in my village. SARVAM's scholarship helped to get the higher studies and fulfil the dreams.

I joined in a Nursing College at Pondicherry. I never thought that I will pursue my higher education but the confidence I gained through SARVAM's life skill classes helped to apply for a college where many students from all over the country studied. I participated in various competitions and won prizes and certificates. I have also involved in a study on "Assessing the Knowledge of Antenatal Mothers regarding Postnatal Diet" along with 7 students which was possible only because of my English knowledge which I gained through SARVAM.

Now I got Nursing Assistant job in a multispeciality hospital at Varanasi and I am role model for other girls who are not ready to come out from the village. I feel that my personality got changed completely. I am able to lead a successful life today because of the possibility thinking sowed in me by SARVAM. I am much grateful to SARVAM-Sri Aurobindo Society of providing me with this wonderful opportunity. SARVAM taught me confidence in lessons such as: Advance with a sense of purpose. Act like a king to be treated like one. The way you carry yourself will often determine how you are treated. For a king respects himself and inspire the same sentiments in others. By acting regally and confident of your strength, you make yourself seem destined to wear a crown. Others tend to follow you. This is a lesson that SARVAM teaches every youth in my village.

needs, and ask deeper and deeper questions on various facets of life. We may call it highly matured-self in common language.

Self-awareness: This entails several elements, such as community cohesion and involvement, cultural activities and leisure, education and life-long learning, health and social well-being, economic well-being and so on. All these are embedded in various activities of SARVAM culminating into a society that experiences enhanced happiness and well-being. In response to a question: '*What kind of self-awareness they think their involvement in SARVAM provided?*' The responses we get are: their courage or confidence, sharping of the focus in what they are engaged in, receptivity, being sincere in perseverance, not indulging in self-lies, humility, gratitude and respecting oneself, one's neighbour and protecting the nature and so on.

Acquired Optimism: Those who know the Mother—personally or through her writings—know that most of these are soul enhancing qualities that the Mother wanted to spread to humanity. This maturity to perceive life with hope, and positivity, rather than fear and desperation is learnt optimism or acquired optimism. In other words, holding an arm from somewhere unknown; developing hope, mustering confidence; and investing one's perseverance to reach where one aspires to reach in life can be called maturity and acquired optimism.

They are expected to become the transformative leaders in the locality, inspiring people to make a difference, rather than being indifferent. They are not easily disenchanted, for they know that their first phase of economic development bristles with difficulties. Initial failures do not frustrate them. Instead, they spur them to more purposeful, determined and dedicated action.

The Augmented Mind's Eye: The trust in the grip of the divine is the true self-awareness. And that the gratitude that someone is playing some role in his/her life to enable them move towards what they aspire for, and value in life is the spiritual maturity. Where does this courage come from? Where does the feeling of gratitude come from? Where does the sharpened focus come from? Where does this maturity come from? For questions like this, one unwavering answer could be: '*This is what we call enhanced levels of consciousness*'.

This is like saying '*we will cross the river by feeling the stones under our feet, one by one*'. *The stones may not be readily visible to our naked eyes. But, one's augmented mind's eye enables one to feel the stones under one's feet one by one, and cross the river of life. This is critical awareness of the self and the social, which is variously called—such as raise in the level of consciousness or out-flowering of the Divine—or handholding offered by the Mother or even use the word 'God' if that makes sense to the user.*

Integral Rural Development: This is the transformation that SARVAM aims at creating—a peaceful one towards enhanced quality of life, breeding humility and gratitude. A life enhancing one, towards well-being of humanity—and the nature humanity depends on. When rural development programmes are the means to achieve this end, the approach adopted is what we call: Integral Rural Development. That which achieves basic necessities of life, and transcends to touch the spiritual side of humans is the essence of it. In the words of Sri Aurobindo, human well-being through improved quality of life, essentially has several elements, one significant among them is: human consciousness.

Adults may be spiritually immature because of early developmental failures. Inadequate nurturing in early childhood causes these individuals to lack a basic sense of trust in others and confidence in themselves. Feeling threatened from within and without, and needing external support, many turn to religion to provide a sense of security and to defend against feelings of inadequacy. Those who progress to higher psycho-spiritual stages have acquired the internal resources that enable them to develop a more mature spiritual commitment.

It has been more than eight years since the previous book on 'Integral Rural Development' was published. The previous version [of this book] explained how 'integral rural development' emerged as unique development practice at small scale. The understanding of the principles this experiment handed down, and the values that went with it, along with the admiration it received from the visitors of Sri Aurobindo Society gave the impetus to expand this experimentation in a slightly larger scale touching several villages, involving thousands of families in many villages.

The rural development approach of SARVAM works like metaphorical touching of a deck of playing cards—falling in a cascade as expected. The central idea was that unfolding the self—not mere income enhancement. It does not work with horse blinders viewing narrowly on improving livelihoods and income. It has higher goals to achieve. Thus, it is away from the conventional/well-known mainstream approaches to rural development.

Every Child is a Promise: SARVAM's approach to work entails, begin with children keeping in view the end in mind that you are going to impact on the entire family. Believe that *every child is a promise.* That

Dharmendran, E., Poothurai, 22 years

I studied in a Government school and I was an average student. My father and mother do not have much education. I grew up witnessing the way life goes in a village, which did not provide any drive to develop any great ambition in my life. However, my thought process got changed after becoming a part of SARVAM's English programme.

When some of my classmates were searching to pursue college education in some local college, I aimed higher. A lesson I learnt in SARVAM was resist the downward pull of the group. The little voice inside me said: stop imitating what others are saying and doing; stop fitting in, and believing what others believe. I applied for Automobile Engineering course at Madras Institute of Technology in Chennai. I got a seat as well.

Perhaps, this is the first time someone from my village got an opportunity to pursue higher education in a reputed institution in Chennai. My parents and friends had a fear whether I would be able to continue my education on a technical subject, all of which are taught in English language. The lesson I learnt and apply in my life is listen to others with respect, but use your own judgements always. Thus, SARVAM classes not only gave knowledge of and skills in the English language, but also enhanced confidence level to survive amongst a fearful crowd in my village as well as a learned crowd in the college. Now, I have successfully completed my 4th year and I am at the verge of completing my degree. I am grateful to SARVAM for all their support. They provided me with necessary tools to analyse life, and to hold a larger perception of life.

Our social personality gets shaped when we operate in groups of people. In the group setting, we unconsciously imitate what others are saying and doing. Often, we are more concerned with fitting in and believing what others believe. We feel different emotions, infected by the group mood. This social personality can come to dominate who we are. Listening so much to others and conforming our behaviour to them, we slowly lose a sense of our uniqueness and the ability to think for ourselves. The solution, I learnt is to develop self-awareness and a superior understanding of changes that occur in us in groups. With such intelligence, we become superior social actors, able to outwardly fit in and cooperate with others on a high level, while retaining our natural-self and rationality. This is a great lesson I learnt in SARVAM, and I apply in my life. I am grateful to SARVAM for revealing this truth to me in a series of motivational sessions. My association with SARVAM not only provided me with skills of learning a new language, but also tools that enabled me have a bolder view of life.

promise can be turned into a great self-propelling force even without the child knowing it. All that is required is discovering the power of the promise; appropriate coaching and mentoring; enabling the parents of that child to recognize what this boy or girl loves doing, which the world needs. Just be available to that child. Don't just hand them any rules. Ask purposeful questions infused with fun. Let them have fun, watch, observe and learn anything in a playful way.

The Immensity of Being Human: Let your focus be elevating their perspective. Let him know: What it means to be 'human' in the first place. What are our responsibilities towards our fellow human-beings, to other species and to the eco-system or the environment? He should not identify himself with limitations. A child should identify himself or herself with the possibilities around. Understanding the immensity of being 'human' is the essence of life.

At SARVAM, children learn lessons through play, songs, drawing and painting, gymnastics, games and conversations. The annual summer camp is the most enjoyed activity-series for children, where specialists working in the sphere of 'child development' come to interact and learn. The experts arrive with their accumulated knowledge on psychology, and skill-sets to work with children on creative activities. At the end of the camp, they have always remarked that they learnt much more from the children than what they believe to have made the children learn.

Children's Well-being

Sl. No.	Points of Analysis and Reflection	Never	Not much of the time	Some of the time	Quite a lot of the time	All the time
1.	I think good things will happen in my life	0	0	0	0	101
2.	I have always told the truth	0	0	0	1	100
3.	I have been able to make my choices easily	0	0	0	2	99
4.	I can find lots of fun things to do	0	0	0	0	101

(*Contd.*)

Sl. No.	Points of Analysis & Reflection	Never	Not much of the time	Some of the time	Quite a lot of the time	All the time
5.	I feel that I am good at some things	0	0	0	2	99
6.	I think lots of people care about me	0	0	0	0	101
7.	I think everyone I have met	0	0	0	0	101
8.	I think there are many things I can be proud of	0	0	0	0	101
9.	I have been feeling calm	0	0	0	0	101
10.	I have been in a good mood	0	0	1	4	96
11.	I enjoy what each new day brings	0	0	0	0	101
12.	I have been getting on well with people	0	0	0	0	101
13.	I always share my sweets	0	0	0	1	100
14.	I have been cheerful about things	0	0	0	0	101
15.	I have been feeling relaxed	0	0	3	17	81
16.	My friends will help me if I need it	0	0	0	0	101
17.	I have a lot of fun with my friends	0	0	0	0	101
18.	My friends are great	0	0	0	0	101
19.	My parents seek my opinion	0	0	46	15	40
20.	My parents show lot of interest in my progress on the ladder of life	0	0	0	0	101

(*Contd.*)

Sl. No.	Points of Analysis & Reflection	Never	Not much of the time	Some of the time	Quite a lot of the time	All the time
21.	My friends treat me well	0	0	0	0	101
22.	My friends are mean to me	101	0	0	0	0
23.	I wish I had different friends	93	8	0	0	0

Like the survey among the adults we referred to, we conducted a quick survey among the children involved in SARVAM's activities for quite some years. This is primarily to know their mind, and how conscious or self-aware they are. Surprisingly, the children have very clear and unwavering answers to many of the questions asked. A good deal of the brain's activities are not apparent to the conscious mind. Thus, their responses were so rapid, one could understand that the responses come from their sub-conscious mind—meaning they are in their very being. They did not have to consciously search for answers. The points of enquiry centred around oneself, and one's interaction with his friend, family and school. The table above shows their responses, which clearly indicates the clarity of their mind, and how they grow up.

Potentials of Children: Consciousness has a second meaning, which is self-awareness. We have been talking about it with many examples in this tiny volume. Thus, children associated with SARVAM grow up with all the liberation to learn, grow and be creative. Being creative is not purely an intellectual process. It may draw on all areas of human consciousness—on feelings, intuitions, and being playfully imaginative, as well as on knowledge and practical skills. The Summer Camps organised by SARVAM is one of the opportunities for the personal growth of children. Children are engaged in various sorts of group activities that aim to explore their talents and the relationships between people and their knowledge (including potentials) of themselves and others.

The Differentiator: Perhaps, the differentiator in SARVAM's approach to children and education can be put across like this. School education often focuses on developing *rational individuals*. SARVAM's approach to education is focused on developing *natural individuals,* while at the same time not undermining the significance of rational thinking for human development. We can clarify the distinction with the following question. *Is true knowledge completely objective independent of feelings?* This is a vital question here for which, rational individuals tend to answer in the affirmative. The implication is that education is about developing a rational state of mind.

Rational Child *versus* Natural Child: SARVAM's approach considers each individual, by nature, are with innate talents, feelings and sensibilities. Education should draw out these qualities. Education should develop the whole child and not just their academic abilities. It should engage their feelings, physical development, moral education, and creativity. They must have opportunities to exercise imagination and self-expression. In this process, education is a process of self-awareness. It points children towards realising their potentials and identifying the element that will elevate their lives. This is about unlocking or allowing them to explore the multidimensional abilities of children. It may help him/her to decide what he/she wants to pursue, or loves being involved in.

As Ken Robinson put it '*education and training are the keys to the future. A key can be turned in two directions. Turn it one way and you lock away resources; turn it the other way and you release resources and give people back to themselves.*' This is precisely about developing every child as a natural individual with freedom to exercise their imagination and creative talents, apart from their academics. The final point is that narrow forms of education, and examination-centric education should not be allowed to marginalise their most important talents and abilities.

By Way of Conclusion: SARVAM aims at cascading a transformational results chain in the service villages of SARVAM. The overall approach aims at transcending the conventional measure of development that is narrowed down to financial terms or in economic sense. It is about enhancement in the perceptions and self-awareness of oneself—the social—and the natural surroundings that provide you the life and livelihoods. Secondly, making the parents pin down their faith in the school-going children. Making them recognise that every child is a promise, and all that is required is providing an enabling environment. Preparing the parents as well as the child to realise this promise is another mission SARVAM is into.

Creating an enabling environment becomes essential in this effort. Any project implemented by SARVAM, on the surface of it, sounds like talking the same sequence of input, output, outcome and impact. Yet, it is deliberately steered for doing the same thing differently. It has vital new components and transformational processes such as sourcing the inner capacities and developing a faith in the Divine—that you get down to doing things with commitment to work, and courage in one's ability, things will mature to show the results the way you wanted.

Thus, the transformational results chain that the SARVAM carries through the entire process of execution is a key differentiator. This approach is transforming households and communities across the villages in this part of the country. As years go by, the area of experimentation keeps expanding, benefiting many more women, children and families. Those involved, became evolved and found their quality of life elevating, express gratitude. SARVAM is grateful to those who support this effort, which make spreading from communities to societies; and from societies across to the states possible.

Chapter 7

Epilogue: SARVAM Rural Development Experiment

Practices that Work and Principles that Emerge

Prof. G. Palanithurai

SARVAM—The rural development unit of the Sri Aurobindo Society in Puducherry has put into practice an innovative concept in rural development. It is called 'Integral Rural Development'. It is fascinating to me, especially because ***(i) it provides a spiritual perspective to rural development practice; and (ii) the approach entails realizing rural development that is human-spirit centric, rather than narrowing it down to the conventional economic sense.*** I explain here my views of the SARVAM Village Development Project. As a student of Political Science involved in grassroots level development work, how I understand and explain this change process, is what I set out to write here.

First and foremost, SARVAM Integral Rural Development is a *process-oriented* project that works at raising the level of consciousness of people, rather than remaining singularly focused on attaining a desirable level of facilities that improve their standard of living. The feature that singles out SARVAM's experiment is that they are trying to improve the quality of life, unlike many regular projects that have the feature of improving the standard of living, as an end in itself. ***The shift of Orientation from target to process has been a methodological imperative to attain the nature of transformation envisioned. Thus, facility improvement is attendant to elevating the real, original self of individuals in the***

community. A notable feature of the initial intervention villages, I must mention at the outset is that one is a *Dalit* dominated Village Panchayat (Poothurai) and the other (Perambai) is a *Vanniar* (Most Backward Class) dominated Panchayat. It is a transformative process that SARVAM put in to action. In the past 4-5 years, this experiment is expanded to a handful of villages in the vicinity. It is spreading by word of mouth, people coming and participating in SARVAM's activities.

The Cascading Effect: The entry point activities or what you touch initially matters in development work. Rural people may not come forward to openly inquire into the purpose of any development work but they are observant. They observe from a distance and try to make out what you are up to. Your initial entry point activities determine how the rest of your activities are going to flow. SARVAM has started off with games and plays for children; supplementary education for children; computer classes, exposure trips, arts, drawing, and dance for children; summer camp for children and so on.

SARVAM focused on children. It did not scatter the activities. It did not overdo things, not having been frightened by the big challenge —rural transformation. Focus plus consistency over a period has worked its magic. Children found these activities interesting and their mothers found it fruitful. The mothers started getting closer to SARVAM, and participating in programmes that involved mothers and children. In a way, the magic touch of children led to an easy touch with mothers, and thus it helped getting in touch with the fathers of the children [men in the community]. Within one or two years, activities for children and women were getting vibrant so much so the youth could not afford to remain indifferent to what was going on. They got their foot in the door of SARVAM's activities out of curiosity. Thus, it cascaded down to the youth in the community as well.

When children get transformed, inadvertently, they become transformers. This ripple effect or cascade—from children to mothers, through men to the youth in the community is interesting. This is the starting of a development engagement of a community clearly in a participatory mode. ***The children have triggered off a participatory wave through their parents which enlists participation from every household, thus, activating massive response from the entire community. It is working on the psyche of the parents through their children.*** Children get transformed. They transform and become transformers themselves.

Instruments of Change: For any change process to take momentum, some instruments have to be brought into play. These could be human, institutional or technological and so on. SARVAM has successfully put to use some (a) 'human instruments', (b) institutional instruments, and (c) informational instruments. It is an integral engagement and not a segmented engagement.

Human Instruments: Children and women at the household level have been used to drive home ideas of nutrition, smokeless *Chulha*, sanitation, cleanliness etc.; and the youth have been used as community level instruments of change. The youth after repeated orientation have started accepting responsibility and played key roles in organizing sports, games and plays. Slowly, they have come to assume the responsibility of managing the day-to-day affairs of the Sathyam Community Centre at Poothurai. Programmes that aroused interest in children and attracted local women have helped make a good entry and gain a firm grounding for SARVAM.

The quality of the transformative change is unique in the service areas of SARVAM. It is both internal and external. The SARVAM team never moved in the path of theory of change. They move with the children and mothers to influence them in their thought process and succeeded in that task. When they succeeded in changing the thought process of the children and mothers, they started orienting them to work on the fundamental transformative change. They are: issues of malnutrition, anaemia, of the adolescent girls, anaemia of the lactating mothers, sanitation and water supply, pre-natal and post-natal care, democratization of the family, respecting the voice of the poor, dignity of the citizens. The very thought process of the people moved from beneficiary to responsible social and development citizens, by taking responsibility at every level through their informed participation. They attach utmost importance in the transformative change aspect in all the activities of the households and the community. A new participatory culture has been created consciously by the people as it has been inculcated as a value. People take responsibility and leadership to achieve development at household and community levels.

Institutional Instruments: Secondly, a range of institutional players such as Panchayats, local committees, banks, hospitals, government departments have played their part as instruments of change. Hospitals have conducted periodical health camps; the locally formed housing committee has identified the poorest of the poor to benefit from the housing schemes; the women groups have identified deserving women for micro credit for livelihood ventures. Witnessing the community discipline at work, the Block Development Office, the DRDA, local banks and CSR Wings of Companies have supported with a host of programmes such as training on livelihoods enhancement, desilting of local ponds and tanks, construction of link road etc.

School Interventions: This actually aimed at improving the academic performance of children have inadvertently earned the teachers a good name from the Office of the Chief Education Officer/District Education Officer, and from community members. It transformed the teachers to come on time and behave like one. ***SARVAM has roped in several institutions to fill development gaps. It has been a win-win situation for everyone who participated. SARVAM did not try to build any forte for itself; rather it has facilitated every institution to deliver their best in their respective field of work—be it education, medicine, sanitation, banking, public works or whatever.*** Thus, SARVAM has been an enabler to fill development gaps without being calculative about who gets the credit. It has given us a lesson on how much an institution can achieve if only they start working in their respective field without minding who gets the credit.

Informational Instruments: Community members, women, youth and children have all undergone a series of orientation and training programmes on general health, livelihoods, nutrition, sanitation and cleanliness, pre-natal care, dental care, care of adolescent girls, expectant mothers and so on. Besides these, capacity building training programmes on goat and sheep rearing, masonry as a livelihood option, specialists talk on cow rearing, motivational talks for children and youth were also held. The village magazine (*Grama Pudiya Udhayam*) has also served as a source of information about local and regional development. ***These instruments [human, institutional, and informational] have come into superb play for change to take place in the SARVAM villages.***

How the Transformation Brims Over? Children find getting high academic grades brings them appreciation; and that achievements in sports, games, drawing and painting etc. are profoundly acknowledged. They get all support from SARVAM to perform their absolute best in schools. They get their role clearly spelled out, that they are supposed to study well, play well, and be disciplined in following the schedules of work assigned at school and by SARVAM. ***This change activated in a child passes on to the mother. The mother gears herself up to be supportive and undergo the right parental orientation, which brims over to touch the man in the family.***

Children's demonstration of excellence in academics, computers, sports and games become a matter of pride for parents. Parents witness their children perform activities that they never imagined their children would get a chance to experience, viz. access to computers; prize for good grades in schools; creative expression through art, craft and painting; recitation of poems and slogans; classical dance and so on. ***They pin all their hopes on the child. They start believing that their dream of getting out of poverty is going to be realized through their child and through their active participation in SARVAM activities. They come under a self-imposed pressure to exhibit their best behaviour to their children***, and to SARVAM. As goodness becomes contagious, parents develop aspirations to do well in life. It can be about the financial discipline to repay a cow loan; or using a household toilet and which weans them off from doing it in the open. Goodness breeds goodness.

[Children's] education becomes the instrument of transformation. Earlier because of the compulsion of the Right to Education Act, it was the responsibility of teachers to make sure children do not absent themselves from school. The SARVAM intervention has shifted this duty as part of parental upbringing.

It is the parents who should make sure children go to school regularly on time. Good academic performance of children motivates the parents to keep an eye on children to ensure they complete their homework before they leave for school the following day. This makes it necessary for school teachers to behave responsibly and spend time in the school productively. School results improve, transition rate goes up and drop-out rate comes down. Local children who had got admitted to private schools in town come back seeking admission in the village government school, which is very unusual in Tamil Nadu. The invisible core that makes all these works is what we call 'transformative process in action'.

Demand Driven: SARVAM did not get down to working with a blue-print for action but with the principle of inclusive development for the *dalits*, for the most backward community and the marginalized. It did not go offering anything on a platter, it has gone on a demand-driven basis. ***Thus the development process has been evolutionary and demand-driven. That there was no pressure to finish any target was a big advantage. The focus has been on facilitating people to make their own search—igniting their inner spirit for action in a search internally towards the principles and ideals they value for an improved quality of life or for a contented living.*** And a search externally towards the basic material facilities that will reduce drudgery in their work and enhance their standard of living, for which people needed to set their priorities and come to a consensus. Thus, SARVAM enabled community groups to deliberate and decide upon their priorities. That means people expressed their demands, and SARVAM showed them how to attain them.

For instance, *housing* for those living in dilapidated houses was a demand; *expanding livelihood choices* to combat vulnerability of poorer households was a demand. SARVAM introduced 'housing' and 'livelihood programmes', and implemented in the way it was locally decided. SARVAM also had to facilitate some needs, that were not the people's priorities, to come into view. Such issues as *sanitation and cleanliness, children's education, men giving up drinking* and soon, which were not their priorities, came into sight only after SARVAM pointed them out. That is demand creation for a good cause. Thus, SARVAM worked 'with the people'—SARVAM facilitated and people participated actively because it was basically their own priorities and in their interest.

Putting the Last First: Touching the lives of the marginalized; and working for the poorest of the poor to elevate them has been the bottom-line of SARVAM's work. The best part of it is making the local people identify those at the margins of the society so as to bring about inclusive development. Local committees identify housing beneficiaries; women's groups discuss and decide who deserve to be assisted first and so on. This is working for the people at the bottom of the economic pyramid and implementing inclusive development in all spheres of intervention. It was possible because the principle of 'we govern and we participate' for general welfare, is in operation. It is not externally driven but is facilitated by external sources. And in the process, many other development players including various departments of the government started lending a helping hand to the people, extending beyond what SARVAM could have reached as the sole facilitator or development partner.

Work at the Cult Level: Any transformative change exercise at the community level has to work at studying and reforming the real culture to an ideal culture or culture that is desirable. What the local culture sanctions positively and what it sanctions negatively are aspects of a cult, which are bundles of values, beliefs and norms. The culture that existed before SARVAM's intervention was that of—'bank loans need not be repaid, which had resulted in banks abandoning these villages:

- we grew up on the streets so will our children;
- school is a place of study for children of educated parents and it's a place where they give free noon meal for the children of daily labourers;
- to drink is manly, and to cook food and give birth to children are woman's work; and
- a woman who questions and argues with her husband has her head messed up and she must be fixed.

SARVAM claims to be a unique project because of the influence it exercises at cult level, shaping the way people think; and the things people attach importance to, and give value for. Valuing the dignity of holding a bank account for instance, and owning a house of one's own and working hard to repay the housing loan obtained from SARVAM; finding the meaning of sending children to school; finding sensibility in listening to and respecting women; giving up drinking in order to repay the cow loan obtained as a promise of improving one's income—all these manifest transformative change—change in their language, behaviour and in their interpretations of desirables and undesirables. ***Such positive aspirations towards life have weaned many men from alcoholism, and transformed him to be a responsible individual in the family and in the community.***

A currency note, meant to be paid as school fees, is lost in the school premises but finding its place at the 'Lost and Found' spot of the school, puts across how cult works at the local school children level. School children going to SARVAM staff complaining that some teachers deny them access to the school toilet or drives them away to use some open space for urinating, illustrates a cultural change. ***All the development transactions are in-built with elements of transformative change process in the community, and which have evolved into a participatory culture.*** The community members wean themselves off the beneficiary mindset, and behave like a development partner with a sense of healthy pride.

Financial Participation: There is financial contribution of community members in every activity they stand to benefit from. There is no free lunch. For instance, in housing there is 30 per cent financial contribution from the prospective owner of the house. Nor is any stamping/marking done in the house or in the toilet—as it is done in many government projects—that it was *constructed with the financial assistance of* SARVAM. This process helps self-respect to remain intact. It communicates that you take rightfully if you fall within the criteria fixed to identify the marginalized. There is no favouritism. It is extending a hand *to the most deserving family* to get lifted through a fair and transparent process. ***Where there is dispute or disagreement, it is left to the community to deliberate, reason out and come to a consensus.*** SARVAM follows the strategy of keeping away in such situations. Since, it is the community groups (local committees) that make all the decisions there is no pointing finger at SARVAM—be it for credit or dissent. SARVAM has made it a point never to force a decision, nor be pressurized by time to be done with it. 'Let them decide and let them own up the decision' is the practice followed, yet watchful that they abide by the principle of bringing the marginalized sections of the society to the centre-stage of development practice.

Nurture the Right Kind of Pride: It follows that from the positive aspirations and transformed mindset of people they get to understand where real pride lies. They encourage their children to participate in school programmes; recognize pride in owning a house of one's own; understand the safety net in rearing a cow as a fallback mechanism from vulnerability; and find sense in women going out of the village for exposure visits to agricultural farms, and so on. They realize that using a household toilet is a matter of being civilized and cultured; and doing it in the open is primitive and shameful. Of course, some realize it sooner, others a little later. ***SARVAM's display of integrity and openness in dealing with people demonstrate its development ethics to the community. People usually hold an ethically-built-development-mirror to be able to distinguish what is sustainable and unsustainable; what is ethically correct and incorrect; and desirable and undesirable in the long run.*** It makes them do a search within one's real/original self. The discussions generated in SARVAM's transactions raise such self-searching-questions. A lesson from SARVAM's sanitation work is that *our sanitation programmes require developing a sanitation culture before providing the sanitation facility* in our villages. Otherwise, toilets constructed through innumerable schemes become useless monuments that serve only the purpose of statistical count and remain unused for the purpose meant.

Democracy and Good Governance at Work: For the ordinary person in India democracy, often, means elections and votes—nothing more nothing less. In SARVAM villages people witness democracy in action and have learnt some of the civic virtues of a real democracy. An easy principle of democracy is: *what the majority have to say*. But, ***in SARVAM villages, it is not who make the majority and who make the minority that matter. It is a kind of deliberative democracy where discussions and debates over an issue (for instance, beneficiaries to be included in a list) keep floating around. The deliberation has to take into consideration the criteria they should not lose sight of in selecting the right beneficiaries.*** Finally, reasoning is used to arrive at the deserving beneficiaries in a fair and transparent manner. It is not without dissents, but the fair and transparent process does not give room for any dissatisfaction to surface. ***It is not a number game (majority winning over minority) but is based on the 'reason and justice' that the criteria draw their attention to. It is a simultaneous engagement of everyone in an integral development process for justice to prevail, through the awakened consciousness of the people.***

For instance, respecting women and allowing them to participate equally in discussions and economic pursuits; identifying the poorest of the poor through a process that is fair and transparent to everyone; parents taking active part in improving facilities in the local schools and child care centres; and financial discipline in the group lending activity—all these go to illustrate good governance in action. Even at the Satyam centre (SARVAM's Community Centre in Poothurai) where children assemble for supplementary education in the evenings, children work on a rotation basis to keep shoes neatly, serve food and so on. Everyone has the freedom to decide and benefit from a given development programme through a justifiably fair process. The purpose is to move to the centre those at the margins of the society in terms of development.

Inspire Absolute Confidence: Where SARVAM is involved in any development work, people have come to develop two important notes of confidence: and (i) there is no compromise on the quality of the work—be it a building construction or nurturing school children to perform to their absolute best; (ii) there is no way money leaks—no corruption. ***The transactions are clean, and there is no greasing of any cog in the government machinery to get something done for the community.*** This has made people develop absolute confidence in the work of SARVAM. Where there is to be community contribution, people do it collecting door to door. It serves as a means of proving the intensity of the demand expressed. This kind of process-oriented ownership has been built.

It has become almost a given, or SARVAM branding, even among government offices in Villupuram district that where SARVAM is present, there is no way of profiteering for private pockets. Similarly, people promptly repay the loans they obtained from banks. This has come about not through any exclusive training, but by the raised level of consciousness on the integrity one must put on view when dealing with public money. Every member of the community takes personal responsibility in proper use of bank loans and in repayment of loans as per schedule. These erstwhile bank abandoned villages are now a priority on banks' list of service villages. Of late, even government offices willingly sanction development works for implementation in the service villages of SARVAM. All bankers and most government offices have become confident of SARVAM villages.

Building the Capacity of the Community: SARVAM's experience also goes to prove a point that ***people are poor not because they are lazy or they do not have developmental aspirations. But because the livelihood skills they have acquired over the years give them very limited choice of occupation.*** Trust and facilitation along with recognition of goodness in everyone can lead to extraordinary results. The poor must be treated honestly and without any damage to their self-respect. They stretch out and walk tall when they get a helping hand, or when they have their capacity enhanced through information empowerment or capacity building training programmes. The Village Development Programme has encouraged individuals to be self-employed and self-reliant, by providing a variety of alternative rural livelihood options, such as dairy units, tailoring, vegetable vending, carpentry, etc. SARVAM has successfully inspired and built the capacity of people to take up livelihood activities that lift households above the poverty line.

Allow People to Claim the Success: ***Success and progress are viewed as the impact of people's participation and the results of their work. Without their whole-hearted involvement, and participation, success cannot be achieved. Their demonstration of faith in themselves has enabled them achieve progress.*** Once they visibly witness development at their household level and in the community facilities, they start believing more. Participation in the development initiatives of SARVAM started flowing in unprecedented measure, bringing in success upon success—for the community as well as to SARVAM. They were made to believe it to be the work of the divine. They were made to believe that 'God helps those who want to help themselves and not those who trust luck and hold a laid-back attitude'. None can punch a hole against truth. Honesty and integrity in development transactions prevail. Almost all the decisions are made by the community (local committees) and so nothing is forced down their throat. Playing hide and seek leads to mutual deception, resulting in grinding poverty only.

Conflict of Interest: It is not that everything falls in place for SARVAM to report success after success. SARVAM has had its own trials and tribulations. The challenges come especially from the political front. The foundations upon which development engagement takes place and political engagement takes place are different. Consequently, SARVAM often faces conflicts with local political activists. Sometimes, even Panchayats take the political side and view SARVAM within tense feelings of rivalry. The development engagement of SARVAM rests on promoting peace and harmony whereas political engagement can thrive only where there is poverty and conflict of interest amongst community groups. Harmony is a potential threat to politics. Political engagement becomes tough when people are after development and harmony. ***When people are absolutely convinced about the works of SARVAM, it proves to be disadvantageous for political parties in the political engagement of people. Therefore, SARVAM is viewed as a potential threat by political activists who often try to sabotage efforts.*** They consider that SARVAM is occupying the space a political party should be using. However, those at this sabotage-game are unable to point fingers at SARVAM on any grounds because all the decisions are made by local committees. SARVAM only facilitates the carrying out of projects and in coordinating with government departments. Moreover, SARVAM deals with these conflicts by behaving as if no conflict exists at all and harmony prevails.

Keeping the Development Mirror Stainless: The repayment rate of group lending activity reported by the SARVAM-promoted-groups are nearly cent per cent. This is an indication of the honesty of the poor. ***The poor are usually honest provided they are treated with honesty. The poor also have dignity and self-respect. They do not willingly become defaulters. But, the mirror [the principle] called honesty must be kept stainless, so that it reflects honesty in the same measure for the poor as well.*** If left unattended it tends to acquire stains from the external environment and it gets too stubborn to remove later on. This principle of honesty reaffirms Mohammad Yunus's (Bangladeshi Nobel Peace Laureate) precept, "The poor are honest provided they are treated honestly".

Creative Expression: Creative expressions of children get communicated through art and painting, or in the summer camps and through computer animations that the children participate in. The community journal, '*Grama Pudhiya Udhayam*' in the Tamil language provides space for local people to write news and share their views on local development. When they see their writing in print, it becomes a material to preserve and feel proud about. ***When they find news about the academic or sports achievements of their children reported in the community journal, they buy a copy and preserve it. They go around showing it to their relatives and neighbours with a sense of pride. They get delight in reading it themselves or to read it out to others and tend to read it again and again in solitude.*** They feel this heightened sense of pride and self-esteem requires sustaining. So, they encourage their children to perform and deliver their best in academics, sports, and extra-curricular activities.

They start showing interest in their children whom they once considered as a pain in the neck. ***The children pay back by doing things that gain the community's respect for their parents. This is exciting and feels great. In order to sustain the community respect the mother has to take care of the children and the father has to exhibit good habits. For the sake of the children the father and mother have got to work on repairing the flaws in their own characters.*** Playing out an unnatural image or putting on a show can be seen through by the child. So, the men and women in the community elevate their characters, filling it with values that they ethically find respectable. It reflects starting from personal cleanliness to repayment of bank loans; and from diversifying livelihood activities to bringing up the children. It goes in waves touching the entire community, transforming how they live. This exercise has proved that development intervention exercises with children can influence the parents [men and women in the community], and thus can transform the entire community. It can bring down poverty levels and heighten the level of consciousness of people.

The uniqueness of the model lives in understanding the integraty of the community. Normally government departments work in isolation.

They work in different perspectives with different strategies and methods. Never they work in convergence with other departments and community, although policies demand it. Nevertheless, they state that they work for the people. This kind of attitude disempower the poor. Further it is not protecting the dignity of the people. Government departments work in the rural areas as long as they have schemes and resources.

The most needed convergence or participatory development is hard to come by in government's style and scale of working. An agriculture Engineering Department do not work in convergence with the subjects of Public Works Department. Rural water supply programmes break open roads to lay down water pipelines. Thus, pipelines are laid, whereas roads are broken. One government department does not work in unison with the other department.

SARVAM will attend to the demands of the people. Basically, it relies on the knowledge of the people. It never imposes ideas unless it is called for by the community. As a result, it keeps the dignity of the people in tact.

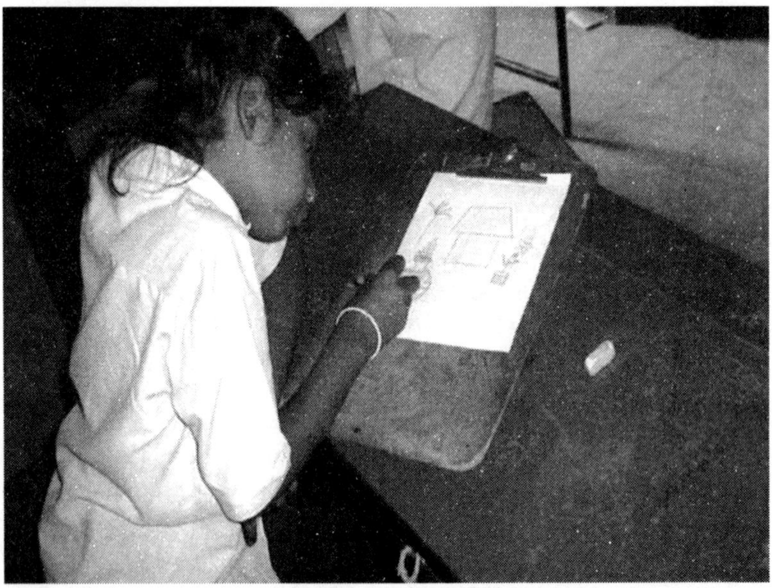

SARVAM perfectly believes in social democracy. Discourse, deliberation, exchange of ideas, listening to the people are basic values of the SARVAM activities. SARVAM works with community in all dimensions and with all segments of the community. It does not have big schemes with huge outlays. It works on ideas, skill, knowledge and activities. SARVAM looks and acts integrally with all segments of the community both vertically and horizontally.

SARVAM's Integral Rural Development experiment has demonstrated how, starting with children, a transformation process can touch the entire community. This could be considered as SARVAM model for rural development. If it works in a set of villages—mostly through volunteers—there is no reason why it cannot work in a larger area in other parts of India or elsewhere.

Index